How to
Read a
North
Carolina
Beach

Orrin H. Pilkey
Tracy Monegan Rice
William J. Neal

How to
Read a
North
Carolina
Beach ∿ Bubble Holes,
Barking Sands,
and Rippled
Runnels

The University of North Carolina Press

Chapel Hill and London

Designed by Heidi Perov
Set in Plantin Light Oldstyle and Triplex

Manufactured in the United States of America

Unless otherwise credited, all photographs are by the authors.

The paper in this book meets the guidelines for permanence
and durability of the Committee on Production Guidelines for
Book Longevity of the Council on Library Resources.

Library of Congress Cataloging-in-Publication Data

Pilkey, Orrin H. 1934–
    How to read a North Carolina beach: bubble holes, barking
sands, and rippled runnels / Orrin H. Pilkey, Tracy Monegan
Rice, William J. Neal.
        p. cm.
Includes bibliographical references and index.
ISBN 978-0-8078-5510-2
        1. Beaches—North Carolina. 2. Coast changes—
North Carolina. 1. Rice, Tracy Monegan. 11. Neal, William J.
111. Title.
GB459.4 P56   2004
551.45′7′09756—dc21
2003014294

11 10 09   8 7 6 5

Contents

A selection of color plates follows page 52.

Preface

Twenty years ago Bill Neal and I began writing and editing the "Living with the Shore" book series. That series now includes twenty-two volumes, one for almost every coastal state. Naturally, we're proud of the series, so every time we're in one of those states near the coast, we seek out the local bookstores to make sure our books are for sale!

Sometimes (I don't want to say frequently, but certainly more frequently than we wish), the book for a particular state is not on display, at which point we move into our book-selling mode. Here is the way it works: One of us sidles up to the counter and asks if the *Living with the [Whatever] Shore* book is in stock. Sometimes it's just a matter of needing to restock the shelves, but if we're told that they don't carry the book, we express shock and dismay and suggest that they should order the book forthwith. We then explain that since we're just driving through town, we can't order a book just now. We don't bother to reveal our connection with the book because we've learned that authors hawking their own writings seem to have little credibility in the eyes of sales clerks.

During this process of scanning bookstore shelves, we've observed—all over the country, in all kinds of bookstores—the range of subjects that pass for beach literature. Most common by far are books about seashells: animated seashell stories, seashell poetry and songs, studies of the biology of shelled organisms, and straightforward catalogs of the seashells that can be found on nearby beaches. Seashell books are followed in frequency by bird books, which in turn are followed by plant books. Clearly, those of us who visit beaches are curious about nature; we want to know more about what we see at the beach. Tourist guidebooks to beaches, beach access, barrier islands, and the coastal countryside also abound, along with popular histories of islands, beach communities, pirates, and ghosts. Shipwreck stories are yet another popular book topic. What we haven't found in these beach reading sections are books about the physical character of the beach—the beach as seen through the eyes of a geologist rather than a biologist or historian. So we decided that a book with the working title "Everything You Need to Know about Beaches except Seashells" was sorely needed. We also decided to focus on the beaches we love the most: those of North Carolina.

Particularly since the 1960s, geologists have discovered beaches. There is an old geologic maxim that says "The present is the key to the past." In studying sandstones that were millions of years old, geologists realized that today's beaches are analogs for similar structures and features found in the ancient rocks. The ripple marks, swash lines, berms, black sand patches, and beach strata provide answers to many of our questions about the world of ancient beaches. Recognition and interpretation of beach features has become standard fare for geology students, and modern beaches offer a field laboratory for sedimentologists. Today almost any sedimentary geology class within driving distance of an ocean or lake beach will take a field trip to dig a ditch across the beach. In the walls of that trench, as well as on the surfaces of the beach and dunes, the student will find strange layering and mysterious bedforms. This whole new world opened up for the geology student is missed by most of the rest of beach enthusiasts. Beach strollers, of which there are millions in North Carolina alone, walk right by these initially mysterious features without looking at their patterns or unraveling their fascinating stories. Shell collectors and birders, beachcombers and casual strollers, are missing these riddles of the sand. What a waste, we thought!

Of course, you can't study beaches and ignore seashells. The shells are one source of the sand that makes up the beach, and a short introduction to the composition of beach sands is included in Chapter 2. Certainly shells hold the answers to some of the mysteries of the beach. For one thing, all seashells, including the "dead" ones, tell a story (Chapter 6). Many of the shells on the open ocean beach came from lagoons. What does that tell us about the beach? Why are so many shells brown-colored? Why are some others black-colored? Why are clamshells usually found on the beach with the cavity face down? If beach strollers knew the whole truth, they'd realize that many of the shells they are collecting—even the bright and shiny ones—are fossils. Some are thousands of years old, a few are tens of thousands of years old, and a small number are the shells of animals that lived millions of years ago.

In this book we just scratch the surface of a very broad subject. We open the door to the world of the physical beach just a crack. Many of the small beach surface features we discuss (Chapter 5) haven't been studied in detail by scientists. When we suggest their origins, we are making educated guesses. This is especially true for the myriad domes, pits, rings, holes, and soft sands made by air in the beach. Curious beach strollers could probably stand in the swash over a number of tidal cycles and figure out a lot of these things for themselves. There are a hundred student projects waiting on every beach. Why does beach sand "sing," and why do some patches of sand squeak while others remain silent when you stride across them? What concentrates black sand? What causes patches of shells to form? What builds beach cusps?

Our friend Sam Smith, an Australian engineer, has visited one beach on the Gold Coast, making measurements and observations at the same time every day for twelve years. He has learned a great deal about beaches; in fact, the ideas presented here about swash-zone "footballs" and how swash-zone orbitals pump air into the beach (Chapter 5) are his. This work has not appeared in the scientific literature yet, and we thank Sam for sharing his hypothesis with us.

It was simply impossible for the three of us to write a book like this and *not* note the deteriorating beaches of our state. More and more, they are being seawalled (with sandbags), nourished with sand transported from somewhere else, and repeatedly bulldozed, all in the name of protecting beachfront property. Of the 320 miles of open ocean shoreline in North Carolina, approximately half is under development. Our view is that we as a society are not doing the right things to preserve our developed beaches for our grandchildren and great-grandchildren. We explain why this is the case in Chapter 7. Beaches are one of nature's remarkable equilibrium systems (Chapter 1), closely related to dune systems (Chapter 3) and part of North Carolina's great system of barrier islands (Chapter 4). We hope this book will contribute to the reader's appreciation of the beach on all scales, from a grain of sand, to a foam track, to the line of wrack that may not be appreciated for the role it plays in the system, to the dune field, to the wholeness of the barrier island on which your favorite beach is located.

We express our thanks to all of the people who gave us ideas over the years about so many aspects of the beach. Foremost among them are the many students from hundreds of beach field trips that we have led. The tendency of introductory students to ask "dumb" yet brilliant questions, unimpeded by a need to appear knowledgeable on the subject, is always a challenge. Often such questions have led us to consider seemingly insignificant beach processes. Just a few years ago, our coauthor Tracy Rice was one of those students. Tracy now works as a coastal consultant, addressing the problems of nourishing beaches. Orrin Pilkey is a James B. Duke professor emeritus of Earth and Ocean Sciences in the Nicholas School of the Environment and Earth Sciences at Duke University, and Bill Neal is a professor of geology at Grand Valley State University in Allendale, Michigan. We extend special thanks and recognition to Robin Park for some of the initial gathering of information and literature for this book and to Amber Taylor for drafting some of the figures. Photos not taken by the authors are credited to the appropriate source, and we thank those people and agencies who provided illustrations. Certainly the publisher of a book such as this has to believe in the value of the product, and we thank the UNC Press for its editorial support. Finally, thanks to our respective spouses, who put up with us when our heads were buried in the preparation of this manuscript, and thanks to my son, Charles Pilkey, for his creative contributions to the figures.

Orrin H. Pilkey
January 2003

How to
Read a
North
Carolina
Beach

one

The Big Picture: Understanding Wind, Waves, and Sand

Walking on a beach in the afternoon sun, while taking in a spacious view of the sea and the mesmerizing waves or scanning the great horizon for signs of life, one often feels that time is standing still. All sense of distance and the passage of time is lost in the fascination of searching for shells or wading through the changing patterns of the swash. For the curious, observant beach stroller, the beach holds many mysteries. Beaches are nature's palette, where colors, textures, and structures change with the variations of waves, tides, and seasons, posing myriad riddles in the sand (Plate 1).

The beach is a benchmark—a scar cut by the edge of the sea into the land. More than the strip between the low-tide line and the land beyond the tidal zone, the beach comprises the entire envelope of sand that extends offshore to depths of thirty to sixty feet, a blanket of sediment interacting with all the forces of the sea, the land, and the atmosphere.

For generations people have associated good health with taking a dip in seawater, and what fisherman doesn't enjoy standing on a beach and challenging the sea to give up some of its bounty? North Carolina is blessed with 320 miles of ocean beaches, ranging down the edge of a long chain of beautiful barrier islands (Figs. 1.1, 1.2).

The Equilibrium That Is a Beach

The key to solving some of the riddles of a sandy beach lies in understanding its equilibrium. The shape of a beach (its width, slope, and general pro-

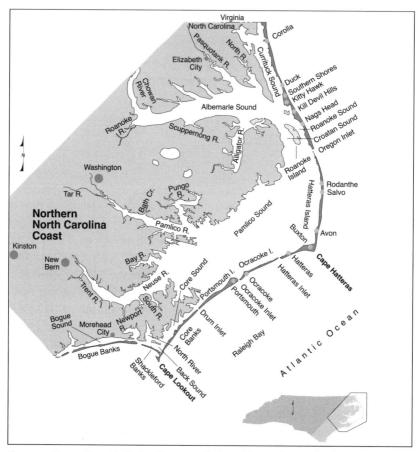

Figure 1.1. The northern North Carolina coast. (Adapted from Pilkey et al., *The North Carolina Shore and Its Barrier Islands* [1998])

file) is the end product of the sea-level change, the quality and quantity of sand, and the height of the waves and strength of the currents. This relationship often is summarized as the dynamic equilibrium of beaches. "Equilibrium" is a fancy way of saying that a balance is achieved between sea-level change, the availability of sand, the energy of waves operating on the sand, and the shape of the beach. When one changes, the others adjust accordingly (Fig. 1.3).

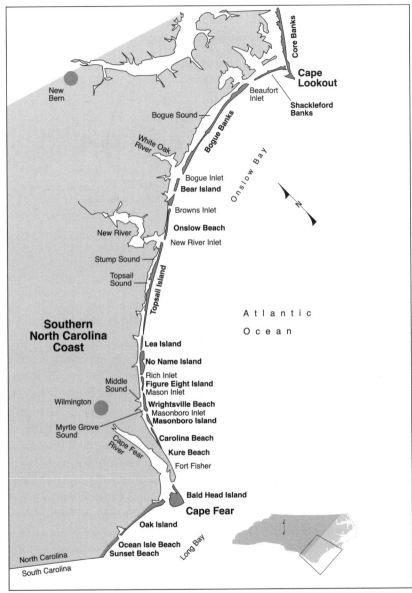

Figure 1.2. The southern North Carolina coast. (Adapted from Pilkey et al., *The North Carolina Shore and Its Barrier Islands* [1998])

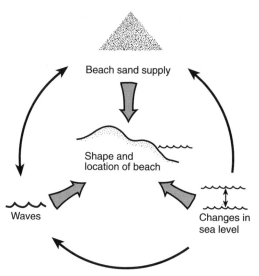

Figure 1.3. The dynamic equilibrium of beaches: When one factor changes, the others adjust accordingly. This is why beaches, if left to their own resources, are very durable. (Adapted from Pilkey et al., *The North Carolina Shore and Its Barrier Islands* [1998])

The constant renewal of the beach reflects the constant evolution of the sea's equilibrium with the shore. The wind generates waves that move onshore, break, and expend energy on the beach. The global pulse of the tide raises and lowers the limit of wave influence on the beach. The earth's rotation, tides, winds, waves, differences in water character, and changing air pressure associated with weather cells all contribute to the formation of currents that act in concert with the waves to move sand. Currents range from great ocean currents that may indirectly influence the coast, to longshore currents formed in the surf zone that cause beach sand to travel for miles, to the local rip currents that threaten swimmers. Topping all of these are the great transfers of energy during storms that whip the surface of the sea into a frenzy of waves and foam. The greatest reshaping of the shore occurs during hurricanes and nor'easters.

Big storms evoke fear in anyone who crosses their paths, but if we stay out of their way (and don't build houses next to the beach), they are not a

Figure 1.4. The Halloween Storm ("the Perfect Storm") of 1991 rolling into the streets of South Nags Head. This storm remained far offshore from North Carolina, and at the time that these huge waves were coming ashore, there was only a sea breeze on the Outer Banks. (Photo by Carl Miller)

problem to the beach or to us. In fact, they are one of nature's most spectacular and awesome sights (Fig. 1.4), ranking right up there with volcanoes and floods.

All in all, the beach is a very dynamic system that is not well understood. Just when you think you can predict natural beach behavior or design a stable artificial beach, nature always throws in a surprise. In the following sections we discuss the sea-level change, wave energy, and sand supply components of the beach dynamic equilibrium.

Sea-Level Change

Tide gauges provide the best record of sea level as it fluctuates daily, annually, and over decades and centuries. From the longest viewpoint, sea level along the North Carolina shore is rising at about one to one-and-one-half feet per century, a figure obtained by taking the average level of the sea surface each year as determined by tide gauges. This may not seem like an impressive number, but considering that the slope of North Carolina's lower coastal plain (the mainland behind the beaches) averages a one-foot increase in elevation for every two thousand feet of horizontal distance (1:2,000), a one-foot-per-century sea-level rise becomes very significant. In theory, each foot of rise should push the regional shoreline back an average of two thousand feet (Fig. 1.5). But it's never quite that simple.

Sea level also changes over the short term in a variety of ways. Storms blowing ashore cause the level of the sea to rise for hours at a time, or offshore winds may cause the level of the sea to temporarily drop. Seasonal wind patterns (i.e., winter/summer differences) or changes related to El Niño can cause rises or falls in sea level that last several months.

The most spectacular short-term rises in sea level occur during big storms. The high-water levels caused by a storm are called *storm surges*, which have been known to raise the North Carolina shoreline water levels more than twenty feet! Such a surge is the result of the combined effects of low atmospheric pressure, mounding due to the circular wind and surface currents moving about the center of the storm, and the piling up of water as it is pushed from the deep ocean into shallow nearshore waters. A storm surge carries sand (and buildings) landward as it comes ashore and sweeps them seaward on its ebb as the storm moves away and the wind reverses direction.

Daily changes in sea level are caused by the lunar tides. In North Carolina, the difference between high- and low-tide levels hovers around three feet. In other parts of the world, the tides may differ by as little as one foot or as much as forty feet. In Pamlico Sound, winds affect water level more than lunar tides.

Everybody, including the folks in states located far inland, is familiar with the terms *low tide* and *high tide* and knows that the terms refer to where the water is on the beach, either low or high. Water levels change as the result of the gravitational pull of the moon and sun on ocean waters. When the moon is located directly over an ocean, the water will mound up due to the lunar gravitational pull. On the opposite side of the planet, the ocean's surface also will bulge as a result of the reduced lunar gravity plus

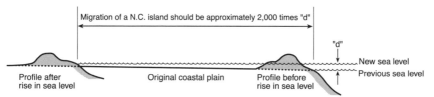

Figure 1.5. Relation between sea-level rise and the gentle slope of the coastal plain, showing why a rise of one to one-and-a-half feet per century (the rate in North Carolina) is very significant. The average slope of the lower coastal plain here is 1:2,000 (for every one foot in elevation there is a two-thousand-foot horizontal distance), which means that, in theory at least, for every one foot of sea-level rise there should be two thousand feet of shoreline re-treat. (Adapted from Pilkey et al., *The North Carolina Shore and Its Barrier Islands* [1998]; drawing by Amber Taylor)

the rotational force of the earth. These two bulges are the high tides, and in between, where the water is correspondingly depressed, the tides are low.

The moon passes any given point once every twenty-four hours and fifty minutes, which means that point will experience two high tides and two low tides each day. Because the moon's orbit is fifty minutes longer than our twenty-four-hour day, the timing of the tides at any beach will shift by an hour or so from day to day.

The positions of the moon and sun relative to the earth change throughout the year. For this reason, the height of local tides will also change from time to time. The maximum is called *spring tide,* when the tidal range on a beach is the greatest. This maximum occurs when the moon is either full or new. The minimum or *neap tide* occurs when the moon is in its first or third quarters. The spring tide at Atlantic Beach, North Carolina, is typically six feet and the neap tide is two feet.

Depending on its orientation and position, a shoreline may experience different numbers and heights of tides. In North Carolina, the tides are semidiurnal, meaning there are two high tides of approximately the same height and two low tides of roughly the same height each day.

Ocean currents also influence sea level. Even currents that are far from the coastline, such as the Gulf Stream off North Carolina, can push water ashore and cause small changes in sea level at the shoreline that last any-where from months to years. North Carolina is at the confluence of the

Labrador Current from the north and the Gulf Stream from the south, so the effects of currents off this state are highly variable and unpredictable.

Over the last three million years, sea levels around the world have repeatedly risen and fallen by more than three hundred feet. When ice covers the extreme northern and southern portions of the continents, sea level is low, and when glaciers and ice caps melt, sea level is high. North Carolina's coastline has extended as far out as the edge of the continental shelf during low sea levels and over seventy-five miles inland from the present coastline during periods of high sea levels. The last low sea level occurred around eighteen thousand years ago. The continental glaciers then melted, and sea level approached its present position around five thousand years ago. Throughout that period, beaches were always present along the landward retreating shoreline.

Sea level has continued to rise very slowly over the last five thousand years. In part, this is because the weight of the water on the continental shelf (formerly high and dry) is causing coastal land to sink. About one hundred years ago the rate of rise accelerated as the result of a number of coinciding events probably related to the greenhouse effect, although it is important to note that the connection between global warming and the greenhouse effect is still controversial. There is, however, no question that global warming is occurring.

Global warming is increasing the temperature of the oceans. Warmer water expands and takes up more space than cooler water, so the present rise in sea level is partially due to warmer water. Global warming also is melting mountain glaciers all over the world and adding water to the ocean through runoff. These processes lead to higher sea levels. When sea level rises, the beach must adjust by shifting landward and slightly upward.

Waves and the Currents They Form

Waves are generated at sea by the wind. Small ripples form on the water as the wind blows across the surface. The size of waves depends on three things: (1) the duration of the wind; (2) the strength of the wind; and (3) the *fetch*, or the distance over which the wind blows across the water. The longer the wind blows, the bigger the waves; stronger winds mean higher waves; and the greater the fetch, the bigger the waves. Thus the biggest waves of all result from the longest-lasting storms with the most energetic winds and with hundreds of miles separating the storm and the beach.

At sea a wave does not actually consist of moving water. Rather, it is formed by energy that is transferred from the wind to the water. This energy propagates, or moves, through the ocean to the beach in the form of a wave. But the water itself is not really moving forward, as in a current. Instead, the energy rolls through the water in a circular motion called a *wave orbital*. The *crest* of a wave is the top of a wave orbital, and the *trough* of a wave is the bottom of a wave orbital. When the wave reaches the shore, it expends its energy by breaking, which in turn moves sand and shapes the beach.

How do you measure waves? The dimensions of a wave are measured both by crest height and by the distance between crests. *Wave height* is the vertical distance from the crest (highest part of the wave) to the trough (lowest part of the wave). Most untrained observers at sea tend to greatly overestimate wave height, which is quite understandable because they do not have any stationary reference points. And then there is the terror factor. A person holding on for dear life in a rolling, bounding vessel is easily convinced of the gigantic size of the waves.

When you're standing on a beach, a good way to estimate wave height is to assume that the surfer you're watching out there is six feet tall. In many cases, the *wave amplitude* is also used as a measurement of the wave's size; the wave amplitude is one-half of the wave height. The *wavelength* is the distance from one crest to the next crest, or from one trough to the next.

Waves travel at different speeds, typically measured as the *wave period* or *wave frequency*. Wave period is the number of seconds it takes for two successive wave crests to pass a given point. Wave frequency is the inverse of the wave period, or the number of waves that pass a given point during a given time period. As the length of a wave increases, so does its speed. In a general way, the higher the wave period, the greater the wave height. Big storms in North Carolina may produce waves with twelve- to fifteen-second periods, while calm weather wave periods are more likely to be three to five seconds.

Local storms with strong winds and small fetch create waves known as *sea.* Sea has an irregular, chaotic appearance characterized by steep, short waves that are unorganized and come from several directions at once. But when a storm is farther offshore, waves organize themselves into *swell,* a less chaotic pattern in which the waves separate into *wave trains* with regular wavelengths, periods, and heights. Swell has longer periods and a smoother appearance than sea. On the North Carolina coast, a wave period of roughly ten seconds is typically the boundary between sea and swell. You can easily determine the wave period for yourself by counting waves while tracking the second hand on a watch.

The wavelength, speed, and period of waves increase with distance from the wind source of the wave train. A mature swell is one that has traveled far from its source, sometimes thousands of miles. As swell approaches the beach, the waves give the ocean surface the appearance of evenly spaced ridges of the same size extending out into the horizon. The 1991 Halloween Storm, now popularly known as "the Perfect Storm," produced extremely regular waves on the Outer Banks beaches (see Fig. 1.4). The waves were generated far out at sea, and winds were blowing at only ten to twenty miles per hour on the Outer Banks as the immense waves from this storm crashed ashore.

As waves move toward shore, they begin to "feel" the ocean floor. In a process known as shoaling, the wave orbitals flatten as the bottom shoals. When waves feel the bottom, they slow down and bunch together (decrease their wavelength), but the time between wave crests (period) does not change. The height of the wave initially decreases when it feels bottom but then steadily increases until the wave becomes unstable and breaks near the beach; the water literally falls over. When they break, waves expend the energy they gained from the wind by transferring that energy to the beach.

Once the waves have broken, they form a sheet of water called *swash.* The *swash zone* is the area on the beach where this thin, relatively smooth, shallow layer of water constantly moves back and forth. As the tides rise and fall, the swash zone moves up and down the beach.

The swash is made up of the remnants of a breaking wave. The thickness of the layer of water in the swash zone depends on wave size and location on the beach. Swash will be an inch or less thick at the top of its

Figure 1.6. Swash lines on a beach in the shadow of condemned buildings and the tilting decks and protruding cable that once led to a house in Kitty Hawk. The lines here are made up of small plant fragments.

landward flow, thinning to nothing as the water infiltrates the beach, and it can be several feet thick in its seaward direction. Some of the swash water returns as seaward-flowing water, or *backwash*, after completing its runup. Swash leaves behind a thin line in the sand called a *swash line* or *swash mark*. These temporary traces mark the greatest landward incursions of the swash (Fig. 1.6). All beaches have swash marks.

The way each wave breaks depends on the slope and shape of the ocean bottom. In general, the wave will break in one of three ways, as a *spilling*,

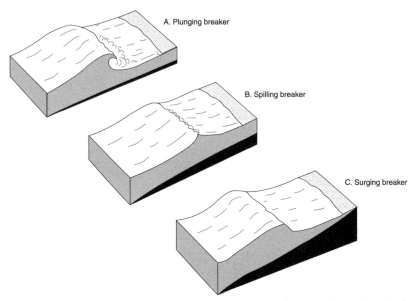

Figure 1.7. The three main wave types on open ocean beaches. (Drawing by Charles Pilkey)

plunging, or *surging breaker* (see Fig. 1.7). Where the beach is relatively flat and wide, spilling breakers will form. Spilling breakers look like they are crumbling as they move along.

With a slightly steeper beach slope, the crest curls over and creates a plunging breaker (Fig. 1.8). These breakers actually form a tube of air trapped beneath the curl. The tube of air is forced into the bottom when the wave breaks, and this air helps to stir up the bottom sediment. A plunging breaker is the sensational, curling type commonly sought after by surfers. Because the energy of the plunging breaker is concentrated in a small or narrow area of the seafloor, it is able to move large amounts of sand.

On the most steeply sloping bottoms, the wave often does not break before reaching the beach. Instead, a surging breaker is formed where the wave surges up the beach and is reflected back to sea. These types of breakers may look just like a series of bubbling mounds of water moving ashore.

Changing conditions alter the beach slope, so all three wave types may

Figure 1.8. A surfer catches a calm-weather plunging wave at South Nags Head in September 2002. Waves on the Outer Banks are higher, on average, than those of southern North Carolina because the narrower continental shelf off northern North Carolina offers less friction to incoming waves from the open Atlantic.

be found on any beach at different times. Often, however, a beach has one characteristic or commonly occurring wave type. For example, the Outer Banks, especially near Cape Hatteras, have the highest and best plunging waves in the state, according to most surfers.

As waves move out of deep water and approach the shore at some angle, the part of a wavefront that enters shallow water first will begin to slow as it feels bottom. This portion of the wave slows down, while the deep-water part keeps moving at its original higher velocity, causing the wave crest to bend or refract. Along most beaches, by the time the wave breaks the refraction is so great that the wave crest typically is much closer to paralleling the shore's orientation than it was in deep water. Since waves can, in theory, approach the beach from any direction, the amount and type of refraction varies widely. Waves that form offshore in the mid-Atlantic may arrive at the beach with an orientation identical to that of the beach. Such waves will undergo little refraction. But waves generated by nor'easter storms, the most common variety in North Carolina, tend to approach the shore from the northeast and are strongly refracted. The wave refraction picture is complicated because North Carolina ocean shorelines may be oriented anywhere between north-south and east-west.

ROGUE WAVES

Rogue waves are spectacular and dangerous waves. These poorly understood waves are rare on beaches, but they do occur occasionally. A few years ago, a rogue wave struck a south Florida beach, rearranging some cars, but no one was injured because it occurred in the middle of the night. As wave trains travel across the ocean from various storms, they frequently meet each other. When this happens, the waves will either cancel each other out or reinforce each other. If the wave crests coincide with other crests, they will have *positive interference*, which really means that the two intersecting waves will become one wave, with the combined height of the two. Likewise, if the waves of two intersecting trains are out of phase, the troughs of one set can cancel out the crest heights of the other. When several waves intersect at just the right time and phase, a rare rogue wave of immense height can form. Such a wave can bury a ship. Off Cape Hatteras, rogue waves have been blamed for the sinkings of several ships.

Currents can also increase or decrease the heights of a wave train depending on the local conditions. If a wind is blowing against a current, wave height will increase. This is why experienced sailors fear a strong wind from the north when sailing in the north-flowing Gulf Stream.

TSUNAMIS

Tsunamis, sometimes called tidal waves, are not generated by the wind like other ocean waves. They are caused by sudden underwater disturbances such as earthquakes, volcanic eruptions, and submarine landslides. The catastrophic release of energy during any one of these events forms a sudden wave of immense wavelength (sometimes hundreds of miles). Traveling at very high speeds, these waves continue to spread out from their source until they encounter an obstacle such as a shoreline.

Tsunamis are extremely dangerous because they travel so fast that there is little time to warn people of their impending arrival. A tsunami formed near Hawaii will take only hours to reach Japan, Alaska, and Washington State. At heights of a hundred feet (thirty meters), an approaching tsunami can suck all the water away from a beach as it nears the shore. Boats unfortunate enough to be afloat in that water will be grounded by the tsunami wave, and unwary beach dwellers have been known to run out onto the newly exposed sand to gather stranded fish. When the wave comes ashore, it does so with such deadly force that it literally destroys everything in its path. People and debris caught up in the wave often get transported out to sea when the water returns to the ocean. No tsunamis have occurred in North Carolina within recorded history; the chance of such an occurrence here, while real, is very slight.

LONGSHORE CURRENTS

Breaking waves form *longshore currents* that carry sand grains (and swimmers) along the beach. Longshore currents form in the surf zone because waves approach the shoreline at an angle (Fig. 1.9). When a wave breaks, a portion of its energy is directed laterally along the beach, and this forms the current. Even a very gentle current can carry a lot of sand because the breaking waves kick sand up into the water column, as evidenced by the discoloration of the water in the surf zone.

The greater the angle between the waves and the shoreline (up to 45 degrees), the stronger the longshore current. This current, sometimes

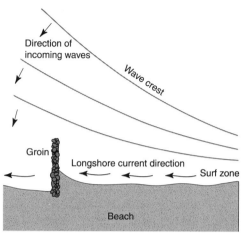

Figure 1.9. Wave refraction. Wave crests approaching a typical North Carolina shoreline bend or refract, causing the waves to strike the shoreline almost head-on. As the waves break, a portion of the energy flows in the direction shown by the arrows, forming the longshore current. The longshore current transports sediment. Structures such as the one shown here interrupt sediment transport, causing downdrift erosion. (Drawing by Charles Pilkey)

called *littoral drift*, is responsible for most of the sand movement along beaches. Most of the North Carolina coast has longshore currents moving from north to south or from east to west (or "down the coast"). *Downdrift* refers to the direction most sand moves on a beach (like downstream in a river), and *updrift* means the opposite direction. Indicators of longshore transport at work in North Carolina include inlets that migrate in a downdrift direction (Oregon Inlet, Mason Inlet, New Topsail Inlet) and the buildup of sand on the updrift side of a groin or jetty (Masonboro Inlet).

Other factors are involved in the genesis of surf-zone currents. For example, winds can either increase or decrease current velocity depending on whether they blow with or against the wave-formed current. Tidal currents can be important as well, but in North Carolina, the tidal component of surf-zone currents is usually restricted to the vicinity of inlets.

A special type of surf-zone current, one that everyone who swims in the ocean should be familiar with, is the *rip current*, sometimes called a rip tide. This is a strong seaward-flowing current set up by the return of water held onshore by longshore currents, waves, and storm surges. Rip currents often flow through gaps in offshore bars and thus may occur repeatedly at the same location. Details about the genesis of these currents are beyond the scope of this chapter, but it is important to note that they pose a significant hazard to swimmers. In North Carolina these currents may become particularly active during and immediately after storms, especially on the Outer Banks. While standing on the beach, you should watch for a telltale band of seaward-flowing water and, if you see one, stay out of the water. Should you have the misfortune to be caught in a rip current, swim parallel to the shore until you work your way out of the current, rather than trying to head directly toward shore. Whenever you swim at the beach, you should be cautious and know what you're doing.

The Sand Supply of the Beach

SAND SIZE

The materials that make up beaches come in all shapes and sizes. Some New England beaches are covered with pebbles, cobbles, and boulders. Beaches north of the mouth of the Amazon River in Brazil are made of mud because the Amazon brings far more mud than sand to the shoreline. But most beaches around the world are made up of sand, including all of the beaches in North Carolina.

Geologists use a grain size scale to describe sediment. The major divisions on this scale, in order of increasing size, are clay, silt, sand, pebbles, cobbles, and boulders. Pebbles are the stones you try to skip across flat water. Cobbles are grapefruit-sized rocks, and boulders are stones too big to lift unaided.

Two things determine the size of sand on beaches: the energy (height) of the waves and the size of the material furnished to the beach. Other things being equal, the greater the average height of waves on a beach, the coarser the sand. This is because higher waves tend to move the smaller grains offshore to quieter water. In North Carolina, wave height generally decreases from the northern part of the state to the south, so southern North Carolina sands are a bit finer in size.

North Carolina beaches are made up primarily of material brought down to the sea by ancient rivers when sea level was much lower than it is now. The sand is composed of individual mineral grains derived from parent rocks originating mostly in the far-off Piedmont Province where Richmond, Raleigh, Greensboro, and Charlotte are located. Grains that survive the long period of abrasion and weathering on their way to the beach are composed of the more resistant minerals. The most common and resistant mineral by far is quartz (silicon dioxide). Other beach sand grains are derived from the breakup of seashells (often 10 to 15 percent of the sand) and come from the ocean rather than from inland.

Silt and clay are the grain sizes that make mud when wet and dust when dry. Minerals of this size, wherein individual grains cannot be identified by the naked eye, are generally the products of the weathering of rocks found far inland, away from the beaches. We rarely see mud on beaches because the waves suspend such fine-grained material and quickly move it either seaward into deeper water or landward into the sounds and marshes behind barrier islands. Layers of mud do sometimes appear on beaches after storms; in North Carolina such beaches include Nags Head, Ocracoke, Shackleford Banks, Topsail Island, Kure Beach, and Ocean Isle. These layers of mud usually contain fragments of vegetation, indicating that they originated in salt marshes and found their way to the beach as the island migrated over them. Increasingly, mud lumps are turning up on North Carolina beaches including Atlantic Beach, Topsail Island, Carolina Beach, and Long Beach. These lumps are the result of beach nourishment projects that used material with too much mud in it.

Dune sand is consistently finer grained than that of the adjacent beaches, even though the dune sand is deposited by winds blowing across the beach. The difference in size is due to the fact that winds generally only pick up and carry the finer grains of beach sand, leaving the heavier, larger grains behind.

Grain size determines the slope of the beach. Beaches with finer sand grains tend to be flatter, with gentler slopes (between the high- and low-tide line) than beaches with coarser grains. The reason for this has to do with the ability of sand to absorb water (porosity and permeability) from wave swash. Fine sand absorbs relatively little water, and so most of the water that flows up the beach also flows back down the beach. This backwash tends to move sand seaward and thus flattens the beach. Coarse sand or gravel absorbs much more of the wave swash, and when a wave breaks on such a beach, more water moves up the beach than moves back down toward the sea. Less backwash means fewer sand grains moving back. In other words, on a coarse sand beach the tendency is for the water to move sand landward and pile it, forming a relatively steep slope.

SOURCES OF SAND

The sand on beaches comes from many sources, including the continental shelf. During fair weather, waves slowly push ashore sand and shells from water depths as great as thirty to fifty feet. Even though the same sand may be partially lost back to the shelf by the seaward movement of currents during storms, the continental shelf remains the largest source of sand for most North Carolina beaches.

Longshore transport is another source of beach sand, carrying it from updrift beaches, sand bars, or tidal deltas. If there are bluffs (as at Kure Beach) or cliffs backing the beach, waves will inevitably erode them and provide sediment to the beach. Along the North Carolina open ocean coast there are no cliffs, but low bluffs or cutbanks form the shores of some of the estuaries and provide sand to their narrow beaches. Dunes along barrier islands supply a lot of sand to the beaches when strong winds blow sand in an offshore direction or when storms erode and cut back the dunes (Fig. 1.10).

Rivers can also furnish sediment to beaches. They are, in fact, the major source of beach material in California. But in North Carolina, estuaries trap river sand miles from the shoreline and prevent it from reaching open ocean beaches. Dams on rivers have a huge impact on California beaches and lead to increased erosion, but dams don't affect North Carolina beaches.

The shells on a beach supply sediment as they are broken up by the waves or by scavengers such as skates or rays (or beach buggies).

An increasingly important sand source on East Coast beaches is nourishment sand dumped there by humans. Many communities now nourish their beaches (Atlantic Beach, Pine Knoll Shores, Wrightsville Beach, Carolina Beach, Kure Beach, Holden Beach, Ocean Isle) by trucking in

Figure 1.10. A July 1999 photo of an erosion scarp on the frontal dune at Caswell Beach. In a natural system, this erosion would supply sand to the beach as part of the natural storm response. But when houses are in the way, the natural beach equilibrium creates serious problems for beach communities. In the background, on the nearest cottage deck that is now exposed on the beach, someone is fishing in the surf zone!

sand from inland sand pits or by dredging and pumping sand from local inlets or from the offshore continental shelf (Fig. 1.11).

Groundwater in the Beach

The beach is the place where land meets sea, and therefore it is also where freshwater meets seawater. Waves bring ashore tons of seawater, while the barrier islands contribute large amounts of freshwater that slowly flow seaward. The upper surface of freshwater within a beach or barrier island is called the *groundwater table*. The position of the water table within the beach has some influence on how much sand will be picked up by the waves and swash; this position shifts with the rise and fall of the tide and may also change depending on recent rainfall. Basically, groundwater can affect sand movement on the beach because of its impact on pore pressure. When the water table is above the swash, the groundwater is flowing seaward, even if the flow is not visible on the beach. This outward flow

Figure 1.11. Beach nourishment at Ocean Isle, March 2001. Almost the entire ebb tidal delta of Shallotte Inlet was removed to provide this sand, shown spewing from a pipe onto the beach. Since the ebb tidal delta is part of the barrier island, one could characterize this operation as robbing Peter to pay Paul, or mining the island itself to save the island.

pushes grains ever so slightly apart by increasing the pore pressure. Grains that are being pushed outward by groundwater can be moved or suspended more easily.

The opposite may occur when the water table is lower than the swash. In such cases, the swash will soak into the sand more easily, and the inflowing saltwater holds the grains closer together, making it a bit more difficult to move the sand grains. The pore pressure phenomenon may influence sand movement on the beach in quiet times, but it is doubtful that it is an important influence on beach change during storms.

One way to tell where the water table is on a beach is to look for *rill marks*, which look like miniature gullies or small streams crossing the beach in the intertidal zone. Water seeping out of the beach face where the groundwater table intersects the surface produces rill marks (Figs. 1.12,

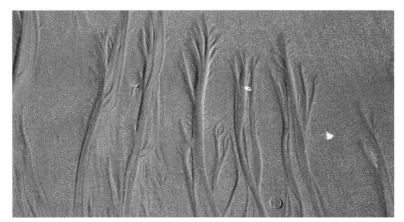

Figure 1.12. Rill marks form as water that flowed into the beach at high tide seeps from the beach at low tide. Usually the water in these seeps is saltwater. The drainage pattern is dendritic (treelike). Penny for scale.

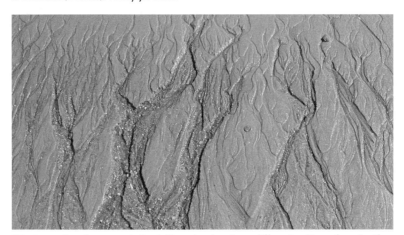

Figure 1.13. A spring 2002 photo of rill marks, showing a different pattern of erosion than that in Figure 1.12. The erosion has exposed a shelly layer just below the surface of the beach. Penny for scale.

1.13). These seeps, which in North Carolina, in our experience, are usually saltwater, commonly form after storms when the beach surface has been moved back by erosion. This shift relocates the position of the water table intersection with the beach surface.

two

What Makes and Shapes a North Carolina Beach

North Carolina beaches come in a variety of sizes, shapes, and compositions. Some are wide and some narrow, some steep and others gentle, some have considerable shell content and some have no shells. If you revisit a beach over a period of time, you will find that the beach width changes and that the slope steepens or flattens in response to some seemingly invisible force of nature. If you know the right places to go, you may find exposed tree stumps on the beach (Nags Head, Yaupon Beach), outcrops of mud layers (Topsail Island, Masonboro Island), or rocks on the beach (Fort Fisher). And although the bulk of the beach is composed of quartz sand and shell, examination of a particular beach may lead to the discovery of a Mastadon tooth or bone fragment (Onslow Beach), sharks' teeth (Topsail Island), giant fossil oyster shells (Topsail Island), chunks of fossiliferous limestone (Shackleford Banks), or smooth, flat quartz pebbles (Nags Head). These fascinating beach forms, fragments, and fossils are clues to the history of the beaches and how they formed.

The Divisions of a Beach

The recreational beach that we all know and love is the strip of sand extending from the low-tide line to the base of the first dune (Fig. 2.1). The submerged beach or *shoreface* extends seaward from the low-tide line to a depth of thirty to sixty feet, where the true continental shelf begins. The shoreface is steep, and a distinct flattening of the sea floor marks its boundary with the continental shelf. The beach itself, both the emergent and the submerged sections, is not featureless. Sandbars and wavy features of huge variety, called *bedforms*, cover the surface of the beach and shoreface. Not only is there an infinite variety of bedforms on beach surfaces, but these forms are ever changing—each tidal cycle reveals a whole new set of features.

Human-made and therefore artificial subdivisions of the beach for descriptive purposes are shown in Figure 2.1.

BERMS

One common feature on the exposed beach is a *berm*, a long, narrow wedge of sand with its steep slope facing the sea (Figs. 2.2 and 2.3). The long, gentle slope behind this steep face actually slopes toward the land. Some beaches have two and even three berms, resembling terraces.

Berms form during quiet weather as sand moves in from offshore. Thus a berm is a depositional feature, one that indicates that the beach has been gaining sand in recent weeks or months. Often the sand making up a berm was once part of an offshore bar that formed in a storm and then gradually, in a matter of a few weeks or a couple of months, migrated onto the beach. The observant beach stroller can actually track this movement of sand on repetitive visits as the bars move closer and closer to the beach. A short time after Hurricanes Dennis and Floyd (1999) passed over the state's shoreline, berms popped up on most of the beaches throughout the state.

Once a berm arrives onshore, it may continue to move up the beach, even to a point above the normal high-tide line, pushed there by either minor storms or spring tides. Meanwhile a new berm may form on the lower beach.

BEACH CUSPS

Beach cusps can sometimes be carved on the outer rim of a berm. These horn-like and amazingly evenly spaced features consist of protruding sections of the beach that alternate with small embayments (Fig. 2.4). Beach cusps give the beach a wavy or undulating appearance. If you have ever walked along the water's edge only to find yourself going up and down a gently rolling surface, you've probably been walking across a series of beach cusps. These cusps are typically uniformly spaced (anywhere from ten to fifty yards apart) and look like scallops from above.

When you are on a beach with beach cusps, you will notice that the

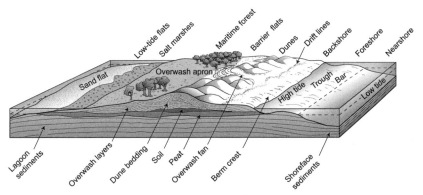

Figure 2.1. Cross-section of a typical barrier island. (Adapted from work by Paul Godfrey; drawing by Charles Pilkey)

wave swash is deflected by the horns into the rounded-out embayments. In this way, the horns are usually gaining (accreting) sand and the embayments are losing (eroding) it. The difference in elevation between the horns and the embayments is usually on the order of a couple of feet or more. Cusps are most likely to form when wave crests parallel the shore, but they are ephemeral features and change shape and size with changing wave conditions.

The sudden appearance and equally sudden disappearance of cusps is just one more mystery of the beach. But if you watch closely and carefully enough, you may be able to shed light on this riddle.

OFFSHORE BARS

Sandbars or *offshore bars* are underwater mounds of sand that may form on North Carolina beaches anywhere from ten to three hundred yards off of the beach. Some beaches have more than one sandbar, with the bar closest to the beach being called the *inner bar* and the one farthest out the *outer bar*. From the beach you can tell where these underwater features are by noting where the waves are breaking (Fig. 2.5), but the pattern of waves may vary according to the level of the tide. Sandbars represent a sudden shoaling of the seafloor that trips the incoming waves and causes them to break. At lower tides, the line of breaking waves atop the bar tends to be more obvious. The waves that break on the offshore bar typically reform

Figure 2.2. A wide beach with a berm crest to the right, a water-filled trough (runnel), and a new berm to the left. The latter berm is a depositional addition to the beach, representing a recent accumulation of "new" sand pushed ashore by the waves. This South Carolina (Isle of Palms) photo shows a much wider low-tide beach than one would expect to see in North Carolina. The great width here and on other South Carolina beaches is due to higher tidal amplitude and the finer grain size of the sand. Note the extensive ripple marks.

Figure 2.3. A low-tide beach at Sunset Beach showing a well-developed berm, also called a "ridge and runnel." This berm is being "welded" to the beach as waves slowly work it ashore. In all likelihood, it will be removed by the next storm.

Figure 2.4. Beach cusps on Carolina Beach following Hurricane Bonnie in 1998. These common features are evenly spaced "horns" separated by embayments near the high-tide level of the beach.

into twice as many smaller waves that break a second time on the beach and run up the beach as swash.

Sandbars come in many shapes and sizes. Some are crescent shaped, while others are long and straight. Wide and low bars may contain a huge volume of sand, while smaller and narrower ones may not contain as much sediment. Bars can extend for miles down a beach, with occasional gaps along the way. Over time these bars move around in response to waves and currents, much like the beaches do.

Sandbar evolution is a characteristic unique to each beach. In some places like Shackleford Banks, the bars form as beach sand moves offshore

Figure 2.5. The beach at Corolla in 2000, with an offshore bar marked by a line of breaking waves. The stumps indicate that the beach is now located where a forest used to be.

in minor storms and then migrates to the beach, forming a berm on the exposed strand. It takes a month or two for the bar to complete its transformation from an offshore bar to a berm. On adjacent Core Banks, the offshore sandbar is more or less permanent and apparently does not migrate onshore.

You can learn how the offshore sandbar works on your beach by making continuous, perhaps daily, observations of its location. Like all things on the beach, just when you think you know the pattern something unexpected (like a storm from an unusual direction) will come along and the offshore bar will do strange things.

As mentioned in Chapter 1, the gaps in bars are often the sites of rip currents, the deadly offshore fast-moving currents that drown swimmers every year. If you can see a consistent gap in the white line of breaking waves, keep away from that portion of the beach even if you can't spot an active current. The gap in the wave pattern indicates a gap in the bar, and swimming there is asking for trouble.

Source and Composition of North Carolina Sand

Beach sand: so common, so complex; so perfect for sand castles, and nowadays a precious and vanishing resource. The expanse of North Carolina's beaches gives the impression of an infinite wealth of sand, but in reality the supply is limited. Except for fragmented seashells, every grain of sand has a long geologic history. Each one experienced a long journey from a distant source, with many stops on the way to the beach. The handful of sand that a child places on a sand castle contains a variety of mineral grains that, under the microscope, are jewel-like—worthy of the castle's kingdom. On the finest scale of beach equilibrium, the size, shape, and mineral density of the sand grains are in balance with the shape of the beach and the dissipating wave energy at the time the grains were deposited. This equilibrium partly explains why grain size and color are so varied on North Carolina's beaches.

COMMON BEACH MINERALS

On the beaches of North Carolina, most of the sand—again not including seashells—is made up of the minerals quartz and feldspar. These grains ultimately were derived from igneous and metamorphic rocks of the Piedmont Province that typically are hundreds of millions of years old. Quartz, the most common mineral, is composed of silicon dioxide, whereas feldspar, the second most common mineral, is made up of sodium, calcium, or potassium combined with silica. Feldspar usually accounts for less than 10 percent of North Carolina beach sand, 80 to 90 percent of which is quartz. Quartz is the most common mineral in beaches because it is very hard and durable and survives both its transport to the coast via rivers and its subsequent reworking by waves better than any other common mineral. In addition, quartz is chemically very stable.

Other minerals disappear rapidly due to chemical and mechanical destruction before they reach the beach. Another durable mineral is the mica, muscovite. Although not as abundant as quartz and feldspar, mica flakes are very visible in beach sand, even when they form less than 1 percent of the grains. The flat flakes lie on the surface of the beach and, on a sunny day, when the grains catch the light angling off the beach, they produce a sparkle, especially in the wave swash zone. However, because mica grains are light and flat, they are easily suspended in water and are usually removed from the beach by waves, to be deposited in deep water beyond the edge of the continental shelf.

Quartz and feldspar are light-colored and translucent, and if they are not iron-stained, the beach will be gray in color. But on North Carolina's natural beaches the sand grains are iron-stained (oxidized like rust), imparting a light-yellow to yellow-brown color to the beach. A large part of the brown coloration of our beaches also comes from brown-stained shells that have broken down into small, sand-sized fragments in the surf zone and have become mixed with the quartz sand grains (Plate 1).

HEAVY MINERALS

Sometimes, patches or bands of darker, almost black sand occur on the face of the beach, most often at the back of the beach (Fig. 2.6). These patches of dark sand are commonly mistaken for the remnants of an oil spill or some other unidentified form of pollution. But the dark sand is very much a part of the natural beach sediment. These patches, found on virtually all of North Carolina's natural beaches, are concentrations of heavy-mineral grains consisting of dozens of different minerals. On average, the heavy-mineral sand grains are twice the weight of quartz. As a result, wind or waves can blow or wash away the lighter sand and leave behind a concentrated area of the heavier dark minerals. When you consider that these heavy minerals make up only 1 to 3 percent of the total beach sand, it is clear that nature is very efficient in creating these concentrations or placers of the heavy mineral fraction.

Sometimes the patches of dark sand are thick enough that you can carefully scrape away a handful of pure "heavies." If you hold such a black sand sample in your hand, you will immediately see why they are called heavy minerals. The weight of the heavy-mineral sand will be greater than an equal volume of "normal" light-colored sand because the dark minerals have a higher density. In extraordinary situations, usually after a storm, the black sand layers may reach a foot or more in thickness, accumulating primarily on the back side of the beach. Dig a hole at the back of the beach. Are there layers of black sand exposed in the hole? Multiple layers may indicate multiple storm events.

Figure 2.6. The black sand on the upper beach at Emerald Isle (summer 2002) is composed of a band of heavy minerals concentrated after a storm. The layer of heavy minerals was generally less than two inches thick. Such dark bands on Bogue Banks often have a purple tint due to the abundance of sand-sized garnet grains.

Multiple layering of heavy minerals occasionally produces one of the more spectacular designs on a beach surface. When an irregular beach surface is truncated or flattened by the wind, the layers show up as a series of bull's-eyes or other complex designs (Fig. 2.7). If present, these are almost always on the upper beach, above normal high-tide level.

When you find heavy-mineral sand on the beach, you have come across a major piece of evidence for where the sand originated. The heavy-mineral composition of sand is a fingerprint identifying the source rock and source area as well as the river that carried the sand to the sea. Different rocks have their own mineral suites or combinations of minerals that are characteristic of the source rocks eroded by a particular river.

Although (as just discussed), quartz makes up on the order of 90 percent of North Carolina beach sand, it typically makes up less than 50 percent of the original source rocks that weathered and disintegrated in the

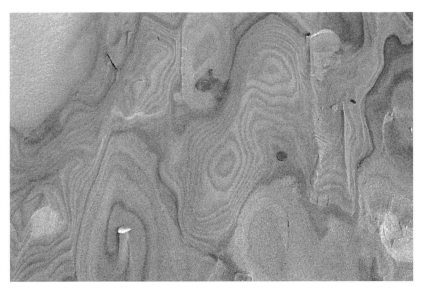

Figure 2.7. Nature's design on a beach surface. This type of feature is found on a beach with multiple layers of heavy minerals. The wind is sculpting the surface of the beach, cutting through the various layers to produce this spectacular art form. Penny for scale.

Piedmont Province to provide the beach sand. The remainder of those source rocks is composed of feldspar, mica, and the minerals that eventually become the heavy-mineral fraction of the beach sand.

For the most part, the heavy minerals on North Carolina beaches are dominated by magnetite or ilmenite—iron oxides and titanium oxides, respectively. Take a sample of dry, heavy-mineral-rich sand and pass a magnet over it. The grains that stick to the magnet are mostly the mineral magnetite. Magnetite and ilmenite are largely responsible for the black coloration of heavy-mineral sand.

A spoonful of heavy minerals from the beach will contain a fabulous mineral collection, but you'll need a microscope to identify the varieties. If the grains were the size of pebbles, the heavies would be a virtual treasure trove. Many of these mineral names will sound familiar because they include some common gemstones. The principal minerals in North Carolina heavy-mineral beach sand (besides magnetite and ilmenite) are garnet, tourmaline, rutile, kyanite, zircon, staurolite, and epidote, plus several types of amphiboles and pyroxenes.

Along the fringes of the black sand patches, the careful observer is likely to see a very slight reddish-brown, purple, or yellow-green coloration. These color differences are caused by concentrations of particular minerals due to the sorting processes of waves and currents. Following hurricanes and major storms, these color patches are particularly obvious and widespread. Reddish-brown and purple colors are due to the mineral garnet (Plate 2). Gorgeous patches of purple garnet appeared along North Topsail Beach after the passage of Hurricane Floyd. Yellow-green colors result from concentrations of the mineral epidote. In a very general way, the garnet-purple coloration is most common on the northern half of the state's beaches, and epidote yellow-green is more common on the southern beaches. Heavy-mineral deposits on beaches can be mined to yield a number of economically valuable elements. For instance, in South Carolina and Georgia, ilmenite has been mined from ancient beach sands (stranded on the mainland by higher sea levels) for its titanium content. In Australia, long expanses of the beaches were mined for zircon, which provides zirconium. Until recently, magnetite was mined on beaches in Monterey, California, for its iron content. Diamonds have even been mined from some African beaches! Probably, if the practice were allowed, most North Carolina beaches could be mined economically for ilmenite.

The heavy-mineral composition of beaches in North Carolina indicates that the beach sand originated in the Piedmont Province, meaning that the sand was transported more than a hundred miles—and sometimes more than three hundred miles—before it arrived at the beach. The Piedmont Province, where Charlotte and Raleigh are situated, includes the headwaters of several large rivers such as the Roanoke, Tar, Neuse, and Cape Fear Rivers. These are all called Piedmont rivers or red-water rivers after the red soil they erode and transport in suspension. The Coastal Plain, as its name indicates, sits between the sea and the Piedmont Province and is drained by smaller, shorter rivers such as the White Oak, Trent, and Newport, which are called coastal plain or blackwater rivers.

In contrast to the rivers of the Piedmont Province, those of the Coastal Plain contain much more zircon and other stable minerals in their sands, evidence of nature's recycling. These minerals are among the "second-cycle" sediments of this region. First the sediment was weathered in the soils of the Piedmont, then it was eroded, transported, and deposited in Coastal Plain sediments (the first cycle), where the mineral grains sat for millions of years. During this time a second cycle of weathering occurred, causing many of the heavy minerals to disappear before they had a chance to be moved to the beach. For a single grain of sand, the journey to the beach is long and arduous. Some grains make it, and some don't!

GRAVEL

Some of North Carolina's beaches have rock (as opposed to shell) pebbles in their sediment. These pebbles are derived from older sediment now being reworked in the nearshore environment, or from offshore rock out-crops on the sea floor. One interesting pebble type consists entirely of quartz that once existed in veins or bands in the original rock. These flattened, oval-shaped, white pebbles make good "worry stones," which every barrier island property owner should carry in his or her pocket. Top-sail Island had a lot of these smooth worry stones on its beaches following Hurricane Floyd. On Nags Head and Kill Devil Hills beaches, patches of small, rounded gravel particles are called "pea gravel." Geologists believe that this gravel, like the pebbles of Topsail Island, is derived from old river beds that once traversed the continental shelf when sea level was lower during the Ice Ages. These deposits now lie beneath the barrier islands and are reworked into the present beach sand as the shoreface migrates land-ward.

Beach Change: A Way of Life

The most spectacular changes in beach shape, changes that can happen in a matter of hours, occur in storms. Sand is often moved from the upper beach to the lower beach by storm waves, a process that flattens the beach. If you have ever visited a beach right after a storm, you probably noticed that it is wide and flat at low tide, wider than you've ever seen it before. Beaches flatten in a storm to spread the breaking wave energy out over a broader zone and take on a so-called *dissipative beach* profile (also called a *winter beach* shape). This defense mechanism prevents the beach from losing even more sand. Between storms and during quiet weather, this sand moves ashore, the beach becomes accretional, and the forebeach steepens. This steepened beach is commonly referred to as a *reflective beach* or a *summer profile* (Fig. 2.8).

Earlier it was noted that grain size controls the slope of a beach between the high- and low-tide lines. This process is operative during fair weather, when the overall beach is steepening as just described. The flattening of a beach in a storm is a process independent of the grain-size effect.

Waves also can push sand from the beaches into the barrier islands. The inland reach of the waves is extended because they ride atop the storm surge or increase in water level caused as winds push water ashore during a storm. This *overwash* sand can be deposited well inland, to the island center or even into the sound behind the barrier island, depending on how big the waves are and how long the storm lasts. Storm winds also blow sand from the beach and into the sand dunes. Dune sand and overwash sand can be distinguished easily. Overwash sand contains large shells, and dune sand contains only sand-sized shell fragments.

During a storm, strong seaward-directed currents can form. Water is frequently pushed ashore by the wind in a storm, temporarily raising the level of the sea; this is called storm surge or *wind setup*. The force of gravity, of course, tries to level the sea, causing a seaward return of water along the bottom. These gravity currents carry sand in an offshore direction.

The opposite happens when the winds blow offshore. The level of the ocean water near the shore drops. The principle of gravity again requires water to flow onshore to level the sea surface. By analogy, this process is like taking a cup of water from a bucket of water. The "hole," from where the water was taken, quickly flattens out. Near the beach this process produces a bottom current directed toward the shoreline. In some cases, particularly on the Outer Banks, strong offshore winds can result overnight in much-widened beaches.

The underlying geology also may control the beach shape or profile. If a barrier island has rocks, peat, or mud underneath it (instead of being a pile of loose sand), these harder sediments may stand out on the underwater beach profile. Just north of Fort Fisher, North Carolina, are some outcropping rocks above the low-tide line. These rocks are made out of ce-

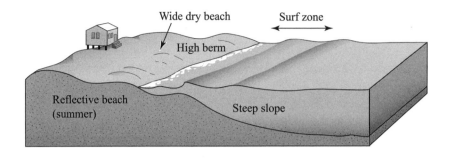

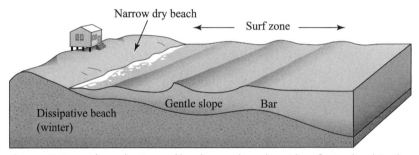

Figure 2.8. Two end-member types of beaches are shown here. The reflective beach is often the summer beach or the beach after a long period without storms. The dissipative beach is sometimes called the winter beach and is characterized by a narrow beach above the high-tide line but a wide intertidal beach. The dissipative beach is a common poststorm beach. (Drawing by Charles Pilkey)

mented fossil shells called coquina that were deposited and buried thousands of years ago. These rocks control where the beach is, its shape, and how fast it erodes.

The features seen on the beach, both natural and artificial, are direct representations of the dynamic forces at any given beach. Each feature, whether it be a dune, berm, sandbar, beach cusp, or heavy-mineral patch, tells a story about what is going on at that beach. These signs can be read; the clues to solve the riddles of the beach. Each beach has to be read in a different way, but the observant beach dweller can learn the "language" quickly.

∻ three ∻

North Carolina Dunes

Beaches do not exist in isolation. Their renewal depends on the interchange of sediment from both the shoreface and the continental shelf on their seaward side and the barrier island dunes on their landward side. In nature's shoreline equilibrium, sand is stored up for a rainy day in the sand bank that we know as a dune. In North Carolina, robust, vegetated, natural sand dunes are harbingers of a healthy beach and vital to the stability of barrier islands. From the extensive dune fields of Currituck Banks to the well-vegetated dunes of Bear Island and the newly forming dune line at the back of Sunset Beach's accreting shore, the beaches rely for sustenance on the dynamics of dunes. During storms, when the sea claims the bounty of the land, these dunes become a primary source of sand to maintain the beach. Dunes also provide critical habitats for a variety of plants and animals.

How Dunes Form

Although they are no more than piles of windblown sand, dunes take on a remarkable range of sizes and shapes, depending on the amount of sand available, the size of the sand grains, and the prevailing wind directions. Over time dunes can grow, shrink, or move in the direction of prevailing winds. Dunes can be created and destroyed by either nature or humans. Dunes can roll over trees and buildings, as has happened at Nags Head and Kill Devil Hills, or be washed away by storms, as has happened on almost all of North Carolina's beaches.

The beach is the sole source of sand for coastal dunes, and every single sand grain in a dune has moved across the beach at some time in its his-

Figure 3.1. A photo of wind in action. The light streaks on the beach are concentrations of sand traveling across the wet beach toward the dunes.

tory. In fact, each grain probably has made the trip many times (Fig. 3.1), because when the wind reverses and blows offshore, some of the grains go right back to the beach. Certainly the prominent *scarp* (see Fig. 1.10), often seen in the toe of the dune after a storm, is evidence that waves have redistributed dune sand back to the beach. Sand can come ashore from both the sound beach and the oceanside beach.

Dune building is helped along by the characteristic onshore coastal winds. Regardless of the general wind circulation patterns of the region, winds will blow onshore at least some of the time, and where there is vegetation, it will trap some of the sand, which eventually grows into a dune (Plate 3). Not only does the sand move, but also the energy of its motion is sometimes transferred to other objects. A glass bottle left on the beach will become frosted as the sand grains sandblast away the shine and clarity of the glass surface.

Dunes commonly begin as piles of sand accumulated in the lee of beach debris such as piles of seaweed (especially *Sargassum*), clumps of salt-marsh straw, and a host of human refuse (fishing nets, bottles, timbers) (Figs. 3.2 and 3.3). Beach debris slows down the wind or blocks it, causing sand to accumulate in the wind "shadow" of the object. Eventually, dune

Figure 3.2. *Spartina* (salt marsh) straw on the beach on Ocracoke Island. The wrack line of straw caused sand to accumulate and now will furnish nutrients to any plants that are seeded here.

grass seeds (especially sea oats) find their way to the new piles of sand, germinate, sprout, and trap more sand. The rotting vegetation, seaweed, or salt-marsh grass that caused the sand accumulation to begin with now furnishes nutrients to help the new seedlings survive. As the plant grows, it continues to cause more and more sand to accumulate. If all goes well and the surf zone stays far enough away, a new dune is born. As the embryonic dune grows, the vegetation keeps moving up and out, holding much of the sand in place.

Dune Types

Commonly, the dune at the back of a natural beach, called the *foredune*, is a ridge of sand forming with its axis, or crest, parallel to the shoreline. Such a dune or sand ridge in association with a beach is also called a *beach ridge*. Vegetated foredunes can be seen on most of North Carolina's bar-

Figure 3.3. Christmas trees piled in front of the dune at Holden Beach in March 2002. Actions like this are taken in hopes that the trees will trap sand and build up the dune, but in general this approach has not worked, and the beach merely becomes cluttered with dead trees.

rier islands and beaches (Fig. 3.4). One exception is Masonboro Island, which is overwashed so frequently that no foredune exists, and a continuous ridge does not form. This is an island in a true state of migration, moving back at the rate of sixteen feet per year. On Bear Island, some foredunes are so active that they support little vegetation, though this is probably a temporary situation. When present, the vegetation on a foredune is usually American beach grass (*Ammophila breviligulata*) north of Cape Hatteras or sea oats (*Uniola paniculata*) south of Cape Hatteras (Fig. 3.5). The vegetation serves as an anchor for windblown sediment and generates continuous dune growth (Table 3.1). When the grass is removed by storms, fire, trampling, overgrazing, or simply too much sand coming ashore across the beach, the dunes are destabilized and may begin to migrate landward, as is happening on Bear Island.

Medaños is the term for isolated large dunes found in coastal areas. Two

Figure 3.4. An overwash pass between low natural dunes on Ocracoke. Sea oats encourage the formation of individual dunes (rather than a continuous line of dunes) separated by passes or low areas that allow overwash into the interior of the island. This penetration of sediment is important, as it helps the island raise its elevation in response to sea-level rise.

Figure 3.5. Sea oats in the dunes near the Old Coast Guard Station on Pea Island in 2002. In the background is the pipe used for disposal of sand dredged from the navigation channel in Oregon Inlet.

Table 3.1. Plants Commonly Found On or Near North Carolina Beaches and Dunes

American beachgrass (*Ammophila breviligulata*)	Saltmeadow cordgrass (*Spartina patens*) Sandbur (*Cenchrus tribuloides*)
Bluestem grasses (*Andropogon* sp.)	Seabeach amaranth (*Amaranthus pumilus*)
Bitter panic grass (*Panicum amarum*)	Sea elder (*Iva imbricata*)
Croton (*Croton punctatus*)	Sea oats (*Uniola paniculata*)
Indian blanket (*Gaillardia pulchella*)	Sea rocket (*Cakile harperi*)
Morning glory (*Ipomoea* sp.)	Seaside goldenrod
Pennywort (*Hydrocotyle bonariensis*)	(*Solidago sempervirens*)
Prickly pear cactus (*Opuntia drummondii*)	Seaweed
Purple Muhly grass	Wild bean (*Strophostyles helvola*)
(*Muhlenbergia capillaris*)	Yucca (*Yucca aloifolia*)

of the state's most famous landforms are medaños: the Kitty Hawk dune from which the Wright Brothers launched their plane and Jockey's Ridge, the largest of North Carolina's dunes and a popular destination for today's hang-glider pilots. Run Hill Dune in Nags Head at the north end of Nags Head Woods, a new addition to the state park system, is another example of this dune type. The spectacular slip face on the south side of this dune is slowly migrating into and burying Nags Head Woods. Wild grapevines, found in patches along the top of the Run Hill Dune, are growing on the tops of tall trees now buried by the dune. Vine growth kept pace with the rate of sand burial as the dune face migrated over the trees. The view from the top of this dune on the sound side of the island is, in our opinion, the most beautiful sight on the Outer Banks of North Carolina.

Medaños, which derive their name from the Spanish word for "coastal sand hill," are a distinctive type of unvegetated dune. These high, steep, isolated sand hills incorporate tremendous volumes of sand and range in height anywhere from tens to several hundreds of feet. Medaños are formed by winds that move sand upward toward the summit from several directions. Despite their lack of vegetation, medaños migrate only slowly, their movement perhaps inhibited by the number of different wind directions from which sand is transported to the dunes.

These dunes are not well understood and may simply represent piles of sand marking locations where there is an exceptionally high amount of sand coming onto the beach. But why should such large amounts of sand come ashore from the shoreface at a particular spot? The answer to the origin of the Outer Banks medaños must lie on the continental shelf, the ultimate source of the sand.

Artificial dunes were added to the state's list of dune types in the twentieth century, when people began to construct dunes in an attempt to hold the shoreline in place. Efforts to improve existing dunes or to create new ones usually include planting dune grasses and/or using "sand fences." The fences reduce wind velocities and cause sand to drop and accumulate in their shadows. They work with varying success. One study in New Jersey indicated that the most important role of sand fences was to keep people off the new dunes, allowing dune plants to prosper. Sand fencing can commonly be seen on Bogue Banks, Topsail Island, and Figure Eight Island and as a component of beach-fill projects such as those at Ocean Isle and Oak Island, where the foredunes were removed by storms or by chronic erosion.

Bulldozing has become a common method of artificial dune construction, in part because the vegetation/fencing approach requires some time to trap sand and build a new dune. On Topsail Island, bulldozers are active throughout the year, continually pushing up sand piles at the back of the beach. We can hardly call these sand-dike features dunes because they lack all of the characteristics of natural dunes (for example, well-sorted and stratified sands that support the growth of stabilizing dune grasses). The granddaddy of artificial dune construction efforts was the old Civilian Conservation Corps (CCC) dune-building project on the Outer Banks in the 1930s. That old dune line is often breached by storms, and new, large, artificial dunes are created to plug the gaps. Once upon a time, even old cars were used to help stabilize dunes near South Nags Head, Rodanthe, and Avon.

The motivation behind artificial dune stabilization in North Carolina has been to fix an eroding shoreline in place. Ironically, new dune construction probably has little bearing on rates of erosion. The amount of sand in dunes is very small compared with the total volume of sand involved in erosion. The retreat of the shoreline is actually a retreat of the entire shoreface, which constitutes a volume of sand many times larger than the contents of foredunes. In the process of erosion, dunes can be swept away and do little to hold the shoreline in place.

Dune Forms and Features

The foredunes of coastal North Carolina form a nearly continuous ridge of sand facing the sea. The size of a dune is mainly a function of sand supply: the larger the supply from the beach, the higher the dunes. Prevailing wind directions, beach width, and time available to build a dune are all part of the sand-supply picture. Most important, however, is the sand available from the sea. So far it is not clear why in some locations more sand comes ashore and builds big dunes, while a hundred yards away the dunes are small and low.

Most foredunes have occasional gaps between them where the storm waves penetrate into the islands. These openings are referred to as *overwash passes* (see Fig. 3.4), and they are very important for the islands' evolution, especially in a time of rising sea levels. Overwash passes allow the accumulation of storm-derived sand, which elevates the islands (discussed below). Today on North Carolina islands, many overwash passes are the result of artificial cuts through dunes at the ends of roads and streets. Even those that appear to be natural were often formed when waves breached a weak zone induced by human activities (such as footpaths or backside notching for construction or a better view of the sea) (Fig. 3.6). When the foredune is very large, like the thirty-foot-high dunes on western Bogue Banks, there are no overwash gaps. Overwash deposits on the back sides of dunes are easily distinguishable from dune sands because of their high shell content. Waves can bring seashells ashore, though winds can't.

Why do some of North Carolina's barrier islands and beaches have many dunes (Bogue Banks), while some have none (Topsail Island and the pre-1930s Outer Banks)? The answer, of course, is differences in sand supply, which in turn may be related to a number of things. Core Banks probably does not have significant dunes because most winds blow up and down the island (parallel to the shore, not across it), which is oriented

Figure 3.6. Beach buggy trails through the dunes south of Fort Fisher. Clearly, unrestricted vehicular traffic is damaging to dune vegetation.

north-south. In contrast, adjacent Shackleford Banks, with its east-west orientation, has some very large dunes because most the winds blow across it. But there are other factors, such as the amount of sand being transported ashore from the shoreface and continental shelf.

Shackleford Banks provides a classic example of the influence of sand supply on dune formation and how ephemeral these features can be. About 3.5 miles from Beaufort Inlet, at the east end of the maritime forest, the character of the dune zone abruptly changes from high dunes with large sand volume to low overwash. From the end of the forest eastward is entirely a migrating, overwash island with only the faintest of foredunes. In places the island looks much like North Topsail Island (without houses, of course).

The high dune to overwash boundary on Shackleford marks a change in sediment supply to the island by the waves that push sand ashore from the shoreface. This was verified by studies conducted by Rob Thieler of the U.S. Geological Survey. Using side-scan sonar to image the sea floor, Thieler detected a sharp contrast in the nature of the shoreface off the two parts of the island. Down to a depth of forty feet, the shoreface off the high-dune western half of the island was smooth sand, but in front of the part of the island that had low to nonexistent foredunes, the shoreface was characterized by abundant rock outcrops and only the thinnest of sand cover. In this case, the nature of the shoreface determines the sand supply to the island front.

Shackleford Banks was not always as we see it today. In the middle to late 1800s, there were high dunes along the beach at the east end of the island that were used by lookouts to spot whales. Harkers Island natives can recall sliding down these dunes on Shackleford well into the 1920s. But heavy erosion has removed all the dunes at that end of the island, and only overwash sand remains.

One way in which sand dunes are eroded is by deflation, a process in which the wind remobilizes sand and blows it out of the dune. The most common feature of deflation is the *blowout*, a bowl-shaped depression with a flat floor that lies below the elevation of most of the adjacent dunes. Blowouts are flat-floored because the sand has been blown away until the sand surface reaches the top of the water table. The wet sand resists being blown away, and the surface becomes vegetated. You can test this water-table control of wind erosion by digging a hole with your hands in a North Carolina blowout. Less than a forearm's length below the surface, you will reach freshwater.

On Shackleford Banks where the high dunes exist, blowouts are common. Some of these blowouts have exhumed old maritime forest growth that was buried and killed by dune migration, although much of the ghost forest has been removed by wood collectors, to be turned into beach mementos.

DUNE SAND AND STRATIFICATION
The faster the wind, the bigger the sand grains that can be picked up and moved by it. Since the speed and direction of the wind changes all the

Figure 3.7. Cross-bedding in a dune in Kill Devil Hills. Two distinct orientations of bedding are apparent, with the upper, almost flat layering sharply truncating the lower strata. Each of the layers visible here was once at the surface of the dune.

time, the appearance of a dune surface varies in texture, color, grain size, and bedforms almost on a daily basis. In the dune, consecutive layers of windblown sand build on top of each other, and over time the layers form a unique type of layering or stratification called *wind cross-bedding*. Cross-beds, which can usually be seen in erosional scarps next to the beach, have several sets of sand layers inclined at different angles (Fig. 3.7). Each single layer indicates a former surface of the dune.

Dune stratification usually consists of hundreds of very thin alternating layers of quartz sand, shell fragment sand, and heavy-mineral sand, plus some layers that are mixtures of all three. The black layers, some only a grain or two thick, are the heavy-mineral strata. Shell fragment layers are usually brown-colored. These layers were each deposited under differing wind conditions. Single gusts of wind can perhaps form some layers, while other layers may reflect wind conditions over a period of time lasting anywhere from minutes to hours. The winnowing of light grains, leaving behind a dark layer of heavy minerals, forms some layers. The surface of the dune that you are walking on will someday be a layer exposed in an erosion scarp at the beach. Perhaps even your footprints will remain.

DUNE GRASS

One dune grass species, sea oats (*Uniola paniculata*), dominates most dunes near beaches in the Southeast. This grass, well adapted to the dune and nearshore environments of salt spray and high winds, slows down the wind, causing flying sand grains to be deposited on top of the grass. Sea oats can be completely buried by sand, but within weeks the plants will break the surface and pop up again. Although they grow well vertically, sea oats do not readily spread and grow laterally. The end result is that they tend to grow in clumps or clusters.

Sea oats are easily distinguished by their long, thin, protruding stalks with grains of "oats" attached (see Fig. 3.5). These "oats" are flat, yellowish spikelets that grow in the summer and fall (from June to November). The stems are cylindrical, and the linear-shaped leaves grow both on the base of the plant and along the stem.

From Cape Hatteras northward, the predominant dune grass is American beach grass (*Ammophila breviligulata*). This grass, too, grows well after being buried by sand. But in contrast to sea oats, American beach grass grows well laterally, and between storms it will even spread out to the edge of the normal high-water line. Oceanfront property owners also plant American beach grass on dunes well south of Cape Hatteras because it grows rapidly and transplants more easily than sea oats. It is best distinguished as the near-beach dune grass without stalks. It also remains partially green during the winter.

Because dune grass stabilizes the sand in which it grows, the way the grass spreads inevitably affects the shape of the dune. Due to the clustering nature of sea oats, dunes that are dominated by this grass will have gaps or overwash passes. Such gaps facilitate the penetration of storm waves onto the island. In contrast, dunes dominated by American beach grass will have fewer gaps, preventing or at least reducing storm overwash except during the larger storms. The penetration of storm waves through the dunes is important because this process delivers overwash sand to the island, raising its elevation. Vertical growth by means of accumulated overwash and dune sand is an important component in a barrier island's evolution in concert with rising sea levels.

Once grasses have stabilized the dune line, additional plants take hold, particularly on the more protected landward side of the dunes. Plants on islands and near beaches require varying degrees of protection from wind and salt spray. If multiple dune ridges form, the swales in between will become populated by shrubs, vines, and small trees, and ultimately, in the succession of plants, a maritime forest may grow. Under natural conditions, the types and density of vegetation are indicators of the age and length of stability of dunes. Grasses may establish themselves within a season, but it may take shrubs ten to twenty years to become established, and decades—even centuries—are required to grow a maritime forest. When a mature forest is razed to make room for development, the vegetative equilibrium is disrupted. Overgrazing by cattle and horses, a widespread problem in North Carolina's coastal past and still a problem on Shackleford and Currituck Banks, extinguishes certain plant species, damages salt marshes, and prevents much undercanopy growth in maritime forests.

The Problems of Bulldozed and Artificial Dunes

In North Carolina, it is legal—with the correct permits in hand—to bulldoze beaches to form "dunes," or at least to pile up sand against buildings for storm protection. Almost every beach in this state that has buildings on it is bulldozed occasionally, usually after storms (Fig. 3.8). Hurricanes Fran (1996) and Floyd (1999) prompted extensive beach bulldozing throughout North Carolina after both storms destroyed many dune ridges.

Bulldozed dunes are easy to spot. These "dunes" have a different shape than natural dunes and often look like large piles of sand that have just been dumped on the beach. These piles of sand contain a lot of shell material, normally a relatively rare component of natural dune sand. After a few days, winds traversing the upper beach will blow away the finer sand grains on the surface of these artificial dunes, causing a layer of shells or "shell lag" to form on the surface. Because winds don't often blow shells

Figure 3.8. Bulldozing the beach to provide a "dune" to protect the houses on Caswell Beach following Hurricanes Dennis and Floyd in 1999. Such artificial piles of sand are usually removed quickly during the next storm.

into dunes, the shell lag is a positive indicator that the bulldozer has paid a visit.

Natural dunes, especially those with roots entangled throughout the sand, provide a solid (if temporary) bulwark against minor storms. When they are attacked by waves, a scarp or small bluff quickly forms. Subsequent waves are at least partly deflected by the scarp, rolling back down the beach and smashing into the next wave coming ashore. Bit by bit, however, the dune scarp moves landward under wave attack.

Helping to reinforce and strengthen natural dunes (in addition to the beneficial effects of plant roots) are electrical bonds, or Vanderwaal forces, uniting the uniform-sized grains of sand and the water between the grains. In bulldozed dunes, which are made up of beach sands with widely varying sizes of quartz grains and shell fragments, neither roots nor Vanderwaal forces can work to stabilize the deposit. As a consequence, artificial dunes erode with much greater ease. The bulldozed sand, minus the animals that once lived there, returns to the beach (usually during the next storm), or, in the case of a low island like Topsail, the dunes are flattened and washed inland.

Beach bulldozing, or beach scraping, removes a thin layer of sand from the inner swash zone (usually a foot or less in thickness) in an attempt to encourage additional sand accumulation. In actual practice, however, the legal limit of one-foot penetration into the beach is often violated, and the scraped sand is pushed to the back of the beach, usually into a low sand ridge.

Bulldozing sand is not good for beaches. For one thing, removing sand from any part of the beach is a form of beach erosion, pure and simple. For another, it kills the organisms in the beach—the mole crabs, the coquina clams, and all the microscopic organisms that live between the sand grains. For days after a bulldozing, seagulls enjoy an unexpected bonanza; you can see them swooping down and grabbing the stranded and struggling critters of the beach that have been left high and dry in the bulldozed dune. The odor of rotting organisms during the postbulldozing days also can create an unpleasant atmosphere for beach strollers. The process affects the whole food chain, including shorebirds and nearshore fish.

The Civilian Conservation Corps Dunes

During the 1930s, the Great Depression was ravaging the U.S. economy. In an attempt to boost the country out of the depression, President Franklin D. Roosevelt devised the New Deal, which included the largest set of government welfare employment programs in history. Included in the New Deal was the creation of the Civilian Conservation Corps (CCC) and the Works Progress Administration (WPA).

The CCC and the WPA looked for projects that could keep large numbers of workers busy, and they found one on the Outer Banks of North Carolina. It was already clear, in spite of the fact that most buildings were then located on the sound side of the islands, that erosion was a real problem. Opinion at the time held that the Banks were in danger of disappearing. At the same time, the North Carolina Department of Transportation wanted to build a highway down the Outer Banks to encourage development in eight small towns south of Nags Head. What better way to solve both problems than to build dunes to halt the erosion and stabilize the islands? The work completed by the CCC and the WPA was the largest dune construction project ever carried out in the United States.

The dunes were built up through a combination of sand hauling by mule, drag pan (the predecessor to the bulldozer), and tractor, the erection of sand fences, and the planting of grasses. The building of the dunes was a well-intentioned effort; in the 1930s no one, at least in the scientific or engineering communities, knew that erosion was part of the islands' natural migration process. It was widely assumed that the ubiquitous shoreline erosion on the Outer Banks represented a fundamental and irreversible loss of island area and that the islands needed saving.

Dunes were constructed along the entire Outer Banks, from the Virginia state line down to and including Ocracoke Island. Of all these dunes built and stabilized during the Depression, many have since disappeared as the eroding shoreline has caught up with them. The beaches are reverting to their old mode of existence. Storm waves are now penetrating into the islands, to the detriment of beachfront houses and North Carolina Highway 12. Hurricane Dennis broke through the remaining dunes in many places, washing out NC 12 near Buxton and destroying several homes and businesses in Rodanthe.

The CCC dune project has had a strong impact on Outer Banks beaches. Back in the 1930s, the beaches were much wider, and they merged into a two-hundred-yard-wide flat island front that was frequently overwashed by storm waves. This sand flat had formerly been the site of important bird-nesting habitats, but it was completely lost to that function. Photos taken from the top of the Cape Hatteras Lighthouse in the 1920s show a large band of light-colored and lightly vegetated sand on the island front, extending as far north as the eye could see. In front of this band was a wide beach.

According to studies by Robert Dolan of the University of Virginia, the CCC dunes have caused beach narrowing and have actually increased erosion rates—the very problems they were supposed to halt! The two-hundred-yard-wide band of overwashed sand no longer existed after the dunes were constructed, allowing bushes and trees that once huddled on the sound side of the island to move seaward, as the new dunes protected them from the harsh wind and salt spray. As the dunes have continued to deteriorate in the face of beach retreat, these bushes and trees find themselves out of place and in trouble.

Plate 1. The beach at Nags Head, North Carolina, showing the typical brown color of a natural southeastern U.S. beach. The falling tide leaves behind distinct patterns on the surface of the beach, such as swash lineation and crescent marks. These structures will be modified by the next tide or by wind blowing in foam or sand. Car keys for scale.

Plate 2. Wind ripple marks in heavy-mineral sand at the back of the beach at Pine Knoll Shores are highlighted by the separation of garnet from the rest of the heavy minerals. The asymmetric ripples moved from right to left, and the purplish to wine-colored, relatively heavy garnet grains are concentrated on the windward sides and in the troughs of the ripples, while the crests and lee faces are marked by lighter grains. The dominant light-colored, light-mineral sand of the dune can be seen in the bank at the back of the photo, as well as in the streak of light-colored sand across the ripple field.

Plate 3. Pioneer plants at the back of the Core Banks beach, along with small clumps of seaweed, interrupt the wind transport of sand. The wind is blowing from right to left and fine sand accumulates in the shadows of the obstructions, creating the embryos of sand dunes. Note the faint wind ripples and the lag of shell debris paving the surface from which the sand has blown away. Both black- and brown-stained shells are visible.

Plate 4. Ring structures of variable size form when the tops of blisters, formed by air forced from the beach, are eroded. The alternate layers of light sand and black, heavy-mineral sand enhance the appearance of the rings. Note that some of the rings are evenly spaced (top center). A strong lineation of sand grains resulted when the last swash swept over this surface (parting lineation), providing a clue as to the water's motion. Penny for scale.

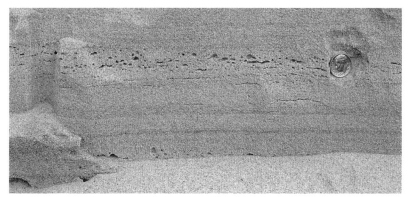

Plate 5. A distinct layer of bubbly sand is exposed in this wave-cut scarp at the south end of Emerald Isle on Bogue Banks (dime for scale). The cavities were formed from air trapped beneath the beach as the sand accumulated. Had you walked on this beach at that time it would have been soft sand and difficult to walk on. The thin, darker laminae are due to heavy-mineral concentrations. The variations in the laminae and beds of this vertical face are like the edges of pages in a book, each telling of different events that took place on this beach.

Plate 6. A field of flat-topped ripple marks on a beach flat records a series of events from the last tidal cycle. The parallel-crested wave ripples formed during the last high tide, but either the current reversed to ebb flow on the falling tide or the wind changed direction. The reverse flow smoothed the ripple crest as sediment was carried offshore (the camera lens cap is resting on one of these flat tops). Note the lighter-weight, dark organic matter trapped in the troughs of some ripples. The entire ripple length does not migrate at the same speed, so ripples sometimes merge, resulting in the Y-shaped junctions.

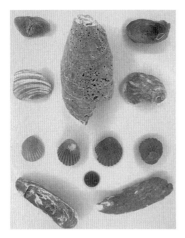

Plate 7. The contrast between brown- and black-colored shells on beaches is striking. The shells on the left were stained brown by exposure to the atmosphere on the beach. The black shells on the bottom and to the right have taken on their color as a result of being buried in mud such as that found in the lagoon. Black shells on beaches, particularly oyster shells, are evidence of barrier island migration. The large brown oyster shell is somewhat unusual in its color, and the holes in this shell were made by boring organisms. Penny for scale.

Plate 8. Students visit the north end of Figure Eight Island to contemplate a riddle of the sand that has to do with human nature: How did we get into—and how do we get out of—this situation? As recently as the early 1980s this area was in its natural state, and beach migration and dune scarping were natural processes. Then the buildings were constructed in the dunes at the back of the beach. The natural processes became a "problem," and the response to hold the line against shoreline retreat has led to beach narrowing, beachfill projects, and sandbag seawalls. (Greg Wolf Photography)

Figure 3.9. Reconstruction (in 2002) of the old dune first constructed along the Outer Banks as a make-work project during the Great Depression. This feature should be called a dike rather than a dune. At this location on Pea Island, known as the "canal area," the dune is regularly breached by storms, cutting off Highway 12. The name "canal area" is derived from the fact that the sand scraped off the road after storms is pushed to either side until the road seems to be running down a canal.

Where did the CCC/WPA project go wrong? Although it was an unintentional consequence, the artificial dune line disrupted the natural equilibrium of the Outer Banks. The designers read neither the indicators of the natural beach and dune processes nor the way the Outer Banks responded to changes in wave energy and sediment supply. These factors favor low barriers that allow storm waves to wash over them and transport sediment onto and across the island, as is the case at Portsmouth Island and Core Banks. Dune formation, with a few local exceptions, was not the natural way on the Outer Banks.

As the system returns to its natural equilibrium, we must recognize that not all beaches are created equal; some get a surplus of sand for dunes and others get overwashed. The National Park Service has adopted a policy of letting nature take its course on the seashore. It has no plans to rebuild the dune line created by the CCC. The North Carolina Department of Transportation, by contrast, is continually rebuilding dunes to protect NC 12 (Fig. 3.9).

When it comes to dunes, nature knows best.

~ four ~

Barrier Islands: The Platforms for Beaches

Every ocean beach in North Carolina, with the exception of Carolina and Kure Beaches, is on a barrier island. Although delicate and even fragile in appearance when viewed from the air, barrier islands are actually both durable and flexible. They absorb the ocean waves that otherwise would affect the mainland. But if the waves are particularly large, the beach protects the island by changing shape to better absorb the storm waves. And if sea level rises, the islands migrate landward, more or less intact.

Islands retreat! What other features on the surface of the earth possess the ability and even the intelligence to escape from processes that would destroy them? We, the authors, have come to view barrier islands in an almost human context.

What Are Barrier Islands?

Barrier islands, by definition, are long bodies of unconsolidated sand, separated from the mainland by a lagoon and from other islands by inlets at both ends. Barrier islands are found on all continents except Antarctica and total approximately 2,500 islands worldwide. Somewhere between 10 to 12 percent of the world's open ocean shorelines are fronted by barrier islands. Around 90 percent of North Carolina's coastline is fronted by these islands, of which there are eighteen (the number could be larger or smaller depending on how one counts them) fringing the coastal plain mainland. Seventy-five percent of the world's barrier islands are in the northern hemisphere. Measuring by length, 25 percent of all barrier islands are American-owned. Using that same measure, 12 percent of the world's islands line the Arctic Ocean. But because the Arctic islands are all very short, they make up close to 25 percent of the world's total number of islands.

On a global scale, most barrier islands remain totally undeveloped. One could purchase large tracts of barrier island land at bargain basement prices in Siberia, on the Niger Delta, or along the tropical rainforest coast of Colombia.

The main types of barrier islands are coastal plain and deltaic. Coastal plain islands line the rims of low-lying coastal regions like that of the entire southeastern U.S. along both the Atlantic and the Gulf of Mexico coasts. Deltaic islands are found at the seaward rims of river deltas such as the islands off of the Mississippi, Nile, Niger, and Indus Rivers. There are no deltaic islands in North Carolina, only the coastal plain type.

There are five components that define a barrier island:

1. *The island.* A typical barrier island extends below sea level to a depth of thirty feet, while the portion above water varies in height depending on whether the island is low and dominated by overwash (Core Banks, Ocracoke Island, Masonboro Island) or has extensive dunes (Bogue Banks, Shackleford Banks, Bald Head Island). An island is made up entirely of sand carried either from the ocean or from the lagoon beach by wind action and storm overwash. Every grain of sand on a barrier island once resided, however briefly, on a beach. On each island we can identify a number of subenvironments such as dunes, overwash aprons, sand flats, salt marshes, and beaches (see Fig. 2.1). Barrier islands, ranging from the tropics to the polar regions, exhibit such great variations in character that it is hard to generalize about them. Padre Island in Texas is so long (135 miles) that it undergoes a climate change and a corresponding change in vegetation from one end to the other! Because vegetation is a major factor in controlling sand movement, the island processes at each end of Padre Island are different as well.

2. *Inlets.* These channels separate adjacent islands and allow the exchange of water between ocean and lagoon—both tidal waters from the ocean and river waters from the continent. On natural islands, inlets open, close, or migrate (on a decadal or millennial time scale). In North Carolina, most new inlets are cut through islands by the catastrophic flow of

Figure 4.1. The 1962 Ash Wednesday Storm flooded Hatteras Island, overwashing the island and cutting a new inlet north of Buxton. The inlet was later closed artificially by the U.S. Army Corps of Engineers and the North Carolina Department of Transportation. Since then small inlets have opened up at about the same location at least two more times. The line along the ocean beach is sand fencing, placed there in an attempt to build up the frontal dune. (U.S. National Park Service Photography)

storm water returning from the sound to the sea during big storms (Fig. 4.1). During the last two hundred years, many inlets have opened and closed along North Carolina's coast, especially along the Outer Banks.

The amount of water that must flow through an inlet is determined by the amplitude of the tides and the volume of nearby rivers. Because the volume of tidal and river water passing through the inlet is more or less constant over time, when one inlet forms another usually closes. In other words, nature maintains just enough openings between islands to handle the local water volumes.

Some inlets migrate (New Topsail Inlet, Oregon Inlet, Mason Inlet) while others remain in place (Bogue Inlet). When Oregon Inlet opened on the Outer Banks in 1843, a lighthouse was built on the south side. The inlet began to migrate southward at about a hundred feet per year, and the first lighthouse soon fell in. A second small light was built only to meet the same fate shortly thereafter. Finally a substantial structure, Bodie Island Lighthouse, was constructed on the north side of the inlet. It remained intact, but within a few decades it had become useless for navigation purposes because the inlet had moved too far away.

Inlets migrate when sand pours into them from longshore currents, forcing them to move downdrift. If there is very little sand in the longshore transport system (as on Bogue Banks), the inlets remain in place.

3. *Tidal deltas*. Huge bodies of sand are associated with barrier island inlets. These tidal deltas are formed from sand deposited by the tidal currents. Longshore currents bring sand from adjacent barrier islands into the mouth of the inlet, and tidal currents then move the sand into the sound or to the ocean side of the inlet to form the deltas. The seaward body of sand, extending into the ocean, is called the *ebb tidal delta* (Fig. 4.2). The sand pushed into the lagoon is called the *flood tidal delta*. Ebb delta size depends on both the tidal amplitude and the size of the waves. The greater the range between high and low tides, the stronger the tidal currents and the larger the ebb tidal delta. The bigger the waves, the shorter the tidal delta. North Carolina ebb tidal deltas extend seaward for distances ranging from four hundred yards to a mile, a relatively short length because the tides are low and the waves are higher than along the barrier islands of adjacent states. Some Georgia ebb tidal deltas are fifteen miles long.

When an inlet closes, the ebb tidal delta is quickly dispersed by the waves and the sand is distributed to the adjacent beach. This happened when Moore's Inlet closed on Wrightsville Beach. Flood tidal delta shoals are not removed after the inlet closes; eventually they are incorporated into the backside of the island and are recognizable as a wide spot on the island. (A beautiful former flood tidal delta can be found on the sound side of Shackleford Banks at the east end of the maritime forest.) When an inlet migrates, the previous channel position fills with sand.

4. *The shoreface* (the lower beach). In front of each barrier island is a steeply dipping, concave surface that represents the innermost reach of the continental shelf. This surface actually forms the lower beach, and the physical and biological processes that unfold there strongly affect the beaches. The shoreface typically extends into the water to a depth of thirty to sixty feet, at which point the sea floor abruptly becomes much more

Figure 4.2. Drum Inlet on Core Banks has a well-developed ebb tidal delta on its seaward side (to the right) and a much larger flood tidal delta in the lagoon (to the left). The rim of the ebb tidal delta is marked by the line of breaking waves. (Mary Edna Fraser Photography)

gently sloping. Fairweather waves push sand landward across the shore-face, providing the sand that eventually forms the beach and the dunes. During storms, large amounts of sand move seaward across this surface. If the storm is big enough, sand may move well beyond the shoreface and out to the continental shelf. This sand is permanently lost from the beach and the island.

5. *The beach.* The beach, which is really the upper shoreface, is like a giant sand conveyor. Every grain of sand on a barrier island once came across the open ocean beach or, to a smaller extent, the lagoon beach on the landward side of the island. Sand is carried either by storm waves or by the wind. Windblown sand may go back and forth between land and sea depending on the direction of the wind. When the beaches are wide and expansive, more sand blows into the islands than when the beaches are narrow.

How Were Barrier Islands Formed?

Barrier islands are the products of rising sea levels. Thus they have been a particularly prevalent landform during ice ages as the level of the sea has repeatedly advanced and retreated across the world's coastal plains. The narrow, subtle sand ridges (sometimes labeled scarps or terraces on geologic maps) that are commonly found on the lower coastal plain of North Carolina are former barrier islands that were stranded when the sea level receded some time in the past. Many coastal communities such as Harkers Island, Beaufort, and Morehead City occupy these onetime islands, which are approximately 120,000 years old. Early settlers in these places took advantage of the safety afforded by their comparatively high elevations.

To illustrate the mechanics of barrier island formation, consider the major rise in sea levels that resulted from the most recent retreat of the glaciers. As the seas began to rise perhaps 18,000 years ago, they first flooded the former river valleys, creating the estuaries and simultaneously causing the formerly straight and uncomplicated shoreline to become highly irregular (Fig. 4.3).

The ridges between these former river valleys then became headlands that projected out into the ocean, making them particularly vulnerable to wave attack. As the waves chewed into the headlands, longshore currents distributed the eroded sands either upcoast or downcoast, forming spits (attached sand bars) that extended across the mouths of the estuaries. Meanwhile the wind piled up large sand dunes at the backs of the beaches, forming ridges parallel to the shore.

Two forces, one catastrophic and one gradual, eventually caused the sand-ridge-covered spits to become islands. Storms breached the spits, cutting them off from their former longshore sand supply. And the gradual rise in sea level in response to melting ice in the high latitudes flooded the lowlands behind the sand dune ridges, eventually isolating them as islands. Similar flooding is taking place today behind the Currituck Peninsula near the Virginia–North Carolina border.

The Currituck Peninsula provides an excellent illustration of this process of island formation; during the last few centuries, twenty-six different inlets—most of them lasting long enough to be named on charts—have cut across this spit that extends south out of Virginia.

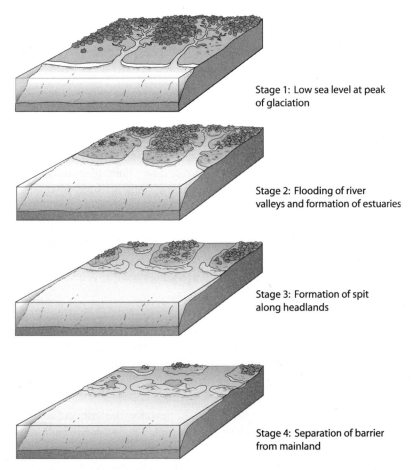

Stage 1: Low sea level at peak of glaciation

Stage 2: Flooding of river valleys and formation of estuaries

Stage 3: Formation of spit along headlands

Stage 4: Separation of barrier from mainland

Figure 4.3. The sequence of barrier island formation. Barrier islands are products of rising sea levels. (Drawing by Charles Pilkey)

Once the sand spits became islands, a whole new set of evolutionary processes took over. The main source of sediment was no longer the adjacent eroding headlands or former ridges, but rather the continental shelf, from which sand was pushed ashore by waves crossing the shoreface or was carried onshore and alongshore from the ebb deltas. Rivers no longer supplied sand to the shoreline because their mouths were miles inland at the heads of estuaries, a situation that still prevails today. As sea level pushed relentlessly upward, the newly formed islands adjusted to their new source of sand and began to migrate landward.

How Do Barrier Islands Evolve?

Barrier islands function like a well-oiled machine. They respond in predictable and sensible ways to all kinds of natural events such as storms, rising sea levels, changing sand supplies, and migrating inlets. In fact, the only enemy capable of doing fundamental damage to barrier islands is the human race. In a technical sense, barrier islands exist in a dynamic equilibrium, just like beaches, involving a number of factors. These factors include waves, tides, wind, sand supply, underlying geology, vegetation, and sea-level change.

Waves are critical to barrier island evolution because they are responsible for carrying sand to the beach from either the continental shelf or from adjacent islands. The importance of this process is shown by the lack of barrier islands along shorelines of very low wave energy, such as the Florida shoreline bordering the northeast corner of the Gulf of Mexico. Storm waves washing over the island bring huge volumes of sand into the interior of the island. This buildup of island elevation is a critical factor in island evolution during a time of rising sea level. The overwash phenomenon was amply demonstrated on many East Coast barrier islands during the 1991 Halloween Storm. In the village of Rodanthe, North Carolina, overwash sediments from the storm exceeded five feet in places.

Coastal plain barrier islands also do not exist where tidal amplitudes are in excess of twelve feet or so. According to studies by Miles Hayes, a South Carolina geologist, tides control the spacing of inlets, which is another way of saying that they control the length of islands. With large tidal amplitudes, a lot of water must flow in and out between the ocean and the sounds, so inlets are closely spaced and islands are short. The islands off the coast of Georgia, where normal tides are around seven feet, are good examples of short islands. Where tidal amplitudes are smaller, requiring less water to flow in and out of the lagoons, inlets are widely spaced and islands are long. North Carolina's Outer Banks consists of long islands because the tidal range is less than three feet. As one moves southward, the tidal amplitude gradually changes and the islands tend to get shorter.

The importance of the wind in barrier island evolution is demonstrated by the differences in width and sand volume of two adjacent islands in the Cape Lookout National Seashore: Shackleford Banks and Core Banks. The dominant winds in this area blow from the north in winter and the south in summer. Shackleford Banks, a wide, high, sand-rich island, is oriented east-west, and for significant periods of time each year sand is blown into the vegetated dunes by the prevailing winds. Core Banks, a narrow, low-lying island with few dunes, is oriented north-south. On most days of the year, sand blows either up or down the island rather than across it. As a consequence, little sand is blown from the beach into the island interior and few dunes form. Like overwash, dune formation is a significant mechanism for building the elevation of an island in response to rising sea levels.

In North Carolina, the geologic framework, or underlying geology, definitely controls the location of some islands and affects the size and composition of their sand supply. On the Outer Banks, stretches of gravel beaches almost always correspond to the offshore location of old river deposits laid down when sea level was much lower. Fossil shells and fossil sharks' teeth are common constituents of some barrier island sands (for example, Topsail Island), all derived from underlying ancient strata. Even the erosion or migration rates of islands are partly controlled by the underlying geology (Figs. 4.4 and 4.5). Islands underlain by mud (formerly from salt marshes behind the island) are prone to more rapid retreat than islands underlain by sand.

Actually, a beach stroller may encounter two kinds of mud on a beach. One is the mud from a former freshwater pond on the barrier island. This kind of mud layer (as on Shackleford Banks and Hammocks Beach) reached the beach when the eroding shoreline overtook the old pond site. The other kind of mud comes from lagoons and is exposed on the beach as the island migrates over the mud layer (Figs. 4.6 and 4.7). Thus fresh-

Figure 4.4. Coquina rock outcrops at The Riggings condominium complex just north of Fort Fisher. This natural rock outcrop was once much more extensive but was mined to provide road-building materials for Wilmington. In front of the condominium are sandbag seawalls, and in the distance is a large rock revetment surrounding Fort Fisher.

water mud indicates erosion, while saltwater mud indicates migration. It is an important distinction, and the two types of mud can usually be readily distinguished by plant fragments and fossil shells contained in the deposit.

Rock outcrops are a common occurrence on the North Carolina shore-face. One large rocky area can be found on the lower shoreface just off southern Wrightsville Beach, and this outcrop may slightly increase the wave energy on shore, because rock absorbs less of that energy than unconsolidated sand as waves roll in to the beach. Another rock outcrop at Kure Beach (see Fig. 4.4) used to be much more extensive than it is today. Years ago it was mined and broken up to obtain gravel for roads in Wilmington.

Vegetation also plays a major role in barrier island evolution. For example, onshore winds blow great quantities of sand into the islands, but when the winds reverse and blow offshore, they don't carry nearly as much sand back toward the sea. Dune vegetation traps and holds the sand in

Figure 4.5. The crooked shoreline at Rodanthe on Pea Island. The crookedness is due to differing rates of shoreline retreat, in turn due to the nature of the rocks underlying and in front of the island. Wimble Shoals, a rocky shallow area just off the protruding part of the shoreline, is responsible for reducing the erosion rate at that point and also for changing wave patterns on the beach. The refracted waves also affect erosion rates. Note the lobate land areas on the backside of the island. These old incorporated flood tidal deltas indicate that there were once inlets in those positions. (Mary Edna Fraser Photography)

place once it gets onto the island. The manner in which dune vegetation spreads seeds and rhizomes is a major determinant of island topography. American beach grass, which is predominant north of Cape Hatteras, propagates in such a way that it causes the buildup of continuous dunes without gaps, as in Currituck. Sea oats, the dominant southern dune plant, tends to form in clusters, and as a result, natural dune lines on southern islands have gaps. The gaps are exploited by storm waves, which wash sand through them and onto the island.

The forests found on the back side of some barrier islands are called maritime forests. These are home to a smaller number of plant species than mainland forests due to consistent high winds and the salt spray from the beach. Evidence of this salt spray can be seen in its pruning effect on the seaward side of the maritime forest, which shows a distinct tree-line

Figure 4.6. A mud layer on the beach at Hammocks Beach State Park. This mud layer is from a salt-water marsh that was once on the sound side of the island before the retreating shoreline caught up with it.

slope down to the sea. On most North Carolina barrier islands, cedars and live oaks are the principal components of the forest flora.

The diversity of vegetation on a North Carolina barrier island depends on the island's size and elevation, which in turn controls the extent of plant exposure to wind and salt. On Bogue Banks, which is wide and has high dune ridges, there are more than five hundred different species of plants. On Core Banks, which is low, narrow, and frequently washed over by storms, the number of naturally occurring plant species drops to a mere twenty-five. In between these two is Shackleford Banks, which has almost three hundred species. Shackleford has high dunes, but the island is not as wide as Bogue Banks. These three adjacent islands illustrate how forest species diversity adapts to the specific nature of the barrier island.

The third major vegetative component of barrier islands is the salt marsh found along the sound shoreline. This shoreline is much quieter than the ocean beach, with significant wave action generated only by storms. The dominant salt-marsh grass in North Carolina is *Spartina*, which is well adapted to the repetitive wet-and-dry cycle of the tides bearing salt water.

Figure 4.7. Another mud layer at Hammocks Beach, showing ribbed mussels and oysters in growth position. Clearly this mud layer was once on the lagoon side of the island. Stalks of dead *Spartina* plants are also visible in the mud layer.

Juncus, or needle grass, is the other common marsh grass; this grass is brown to black compared to *Spartina*'s green color in the growing season. *Juncus* cannot tolerate daily salt-water inundation as *Spartina* can, so it lives on the upland side of the marsh.

The thick congregation of marsh grasses baffles the little wave energy that does strike the sound shoreline, trapping the sediment from the water much like dune grasses trap it from the air. The marshes build up mud, windblown sand, and peat as the grasses grow, trap sediments, die, and are buried, eventually to become part of the island above sea level (Figs. 4.8 and 4.9).

As already mentioned, barrier islands are products of rising sea levels. No sea-level rise would mean that no valleys were flooded to form estuaries, and no islands would be built across the mouths of estuaries.

Figure 4.8. The east end of Ocracoke, showing the rim of salt marsh along the lagoon side of the island. Also visible in the photo are Highway 12 and, in the distance, the outline of the ebb tidal delta of Hatteras Inlet. Salt marsh is a critical habitat for a number of marine organisms and also slows down shoreline retreat on the lagoon shore. (Mary Edna Fraser Photography)

Figure 4.9. *Spartina* salt marsh behind Lea Island at high tide. True salt marsh requires inundation by saltwater on a daily basis. This photo was taken from a tidal creek looking toward the mainland.

Barrier Island Migration

Essentially all the barrier islands in the world are "eroding," but they are not disappearing. This erosion is part of the barrier island migration process that occurs in response to changing sea level and coastal evolution.

Island migration is an amazing geologic phenomenon that was not even recognized until the early 1960s, when it was finally brought to light, almost simultaneously, by three graduate students studying the Outer Banks of North Carolina: John Fisher of the University of North Carolina at Chapel Hill, Paul Godfrey of Duke University, and Bob Dolan of Louisiana State University. Their discovery changed coastal science and coastal management in a big way.

During the 1930s and 1940s, shoreline erosion was very evident on the Outer Banks, and the Civilian Conservation Corps began a massive dune-building effort to save the islands (see Chapter 3). The resulting continuous artificial dune line reached almost from the Virginia border to Ocracoke Island, well below Cape Hatteras (see Chapter 6). This protective dune wall made perfect sense in the context of the prevailing ideas about

Figure 4.10. Overwash on Core Banks after Hurricane Dennis in 1999. Dennis was a relatively small storm, but its waves were just the right size to overwash much of the island. In bigger storms, the waves either break far offshore or sometimes pass completely over the island, leaving relatively little sand behind.

barrier islands at the time. But Fisher, Godfrey, and Dolan proved that the islands were *not*, in fact, eroding away. Instead the islands were actually migrating, and shoreline erosion was a natural part of that process. This major discovery later prompted the National Park Service to announce that henceforth it would keep its hands off the islands and let nature rip.

Island migration involves three fundamental processes: (1) open ocean shoreline retreat; (2) lagoonside widening of the island by overwash on the sound shoreline; and (3) elevation of the central part of the island by overwash (Fig. 4.10).

Oceanside shoreline retreat is due to a number of factors, some of which remain unknown. These factors include myriad human activities that affect sand supplies, plus the ongoing sea-level rise. Lagoonside widening is also carried out via a number of processes, particularly overwash and the incorporation of tidal deltas. On Masonboro Island, storm waves from Hurricane Fran washed over the narrow (less than 300 feet wide) island and deposited a series of sand fans on the salt marsh behind it, thus widening the entire island in a matter of hours. This is the only North Carolina island that is in a complete state of migration (Fig. 4.11).

Figure 4.11. Ghostly trees on Masonboro Island. This is the only island in North Carolina that is migrating toward the mainland in its entirety. It is moving back at approximately sixteen feet per year.

As we have emphasized elsewhere, a key element in island migration and evolution is sand supply. A continuous diet of fresh sand is needed to maintain migrating islands. Much of this sand comes from deposits of former river sand, once found at the heads of estuaries that lay seaward of the present shore when sea level was lower. The quartz grains and heavy minerals on our present-day beaches were once river sediments, but sea-level rise and related barrier island migration have caused today's waves to wash over yesterday's estuaries, sweeping up the sand particles and reincorporating them into the barrier islands and beaches on which we walk.

In some instances, particularly on Cedar and Masonboro Islands, Caswell Beach, Holden Beach, and Ocean Isle, salt-marsh muds formed on the lagoon side of the island crop out extensively on the beach. Ocracoke and Topsail Islands both had outcrops of marsh sediments exposed on their beaches following Hurricane Floyd. These occurrences, as well as the ubiquitous presence of oyster shells on many barrier island beaches (Ocracoke, Onslow Beach, Topsail Island, Wrightsville Beach, Holden Beach, Ocean Isle), offer the best proof that barrier island migration is for real.

Needless to say, the mainland shoreline must itself move back as islands migrate, or the islands will no longer be islands. In fact, once in a while migrating islands do catch up with and attach to the mainland. This is what has happened at Myrtle Beach, South Carolina, as well as at Kure Beach and Carolina Beach, North Carolina. In these places the mainland fronts the open ocean.

What's Happening Today?

Something fundamental has been taking place within the last hundred years or so: Virtually all coastal plain barrier islands in the world are eroding. On islands with open water and little salt marsh behind them (such as Pea, Hatteras, and Ocracoke Islands and Shackleford Banks), erosion is occurring on the lagoon side as well as the ocean side. The barrier islands are slimming down, even those that were building seaward just a century ago.

Two causes have been suggested for the narrowing of barrier islands. Humans are certainly involved. By damming rivers, jettying inlets, seawalling beaches, and dredging channels and harbors, they have precipitated a sand-supply crisis. This shortage of sand is causing worldwide erosion. The most fundamental cause of barrier island narrowing, however, is very likely a natural one: the rise in the level of the sea. Evidence for this position is provided by the fact that islands on our national seashores and islands elsewhere in the world where human impact is light are rapidly thinning along with their more developed cousins. Thinning is nature's way of facilitating island migration. Thin islands allow the frequent cross-island overwash necessary for efficient and rapid island migration in the future. Only narrow islands (like Masonboro Island) can migrate rapidly. Putting it another way, the islands are sensing the sea-level rise, and the first step in preparing to migrate is island thinning.

five

Beach Clues: Reading the Signs on the Beach

North Carolina's beaches are in a constant state of change, and reading the clues to understand these changes is every bit as challenging as detective work. Storms leave the most obvious signs of their visits, but daily winds, waves, and tides make their marks as well. Each process on the beach leaves a fingerprint. Clues on or within the beach will give you access to a record of events that may have happened months ago or others that might be happening as you are watching! This chapter examines features associated with processes as great as storms and as minute as the gentle bouncing of a windblown ball of foam across the sand. Most of us aren't likely to be on the beach during a storm (unless you're one of those diehard surfers), when the sea surface is whipped into a froth and the waves run up onto the back of the beach and into the dunes. But the evidence of sea foam, ripple marks in the sand, and especially the storm's debris-line deposits are visible for some time after the storm has passed.

Drift and Wrack Lines

Who doesn't have a story or a favorite memory of finding something unexpected that drifted up on a beach? We ourselves have "discovered" shipwreck timbers, glass net floats from exotic places, strange liquor bottles from foreign countries (including Russia, China, the U.K., Spain, Germany, Norway, Canada, and Brazil), whale bones and baleen, tar balls from oil spills, sharks' teeth, and of course a huge variety of seashells, both fossil and modern. Some of those imported beer bottles have onshore origins, being left behind by careless beach users. We have discovered a num-

Figure 5.1. Sooner or later, everything winds up on a beach. This bloated dead whale washed up on South Nags Head in 1993. It came ashore during strong onshore winds.

ber of bottles with messages inside them. But they all came from nearby beach communities or adjacent islands, and some of the messages indicated that the writer probably consumed the contents of the bottle before taking pen in hand. The senior author of this book, Orrin Pilkey, once was lecturing to a class on the beach at South Nags Head when he noticed that the students' attention was being diverted (more than usual). It turned out that a dead whale had just floated ashore a few tens of yards from where they stood (Fig. 5.1). Regardless of its origins, the waves concentrate all debris into the high-water mark.

Much of the extraneous material on beaches is found in *drift lines* (*wrack lines*), which are the linear piles of natural and artificial objects left behind at the uppermost limit of the wave swash (Fig. 5.2). The positions of drift lines are a good indicator of the high-tide or storm-wave limit. On some North Carolina beaches, especially the undisturbed ones in our

Figure 5.2. A wrack line of *Spartina* (salt marsh) straw and wood from destroyed decks and dune walkovers in South Nags Head during a nor'easter in 1998. The Comfort Inn at Whalebone Junction is in the background.

parks and National Seashores, as many as three separate wrack lines can sometimes be seen. The lowest line of debris marks the normal high-tide line. The next, a foot or two higher, is from the last spring or full-moon tide, and the highest is from the last big storm. A walk into the dunes, into the center of the island far from the shoreline, may reveal old lines left from significant flooding due to a nor'easter or hurricane as long as ten or twenty years ago.

A significant part of the human-made flotsam and jetsam in drift lines originates offshore. Containers of alcoholic drinks seem most prevalent, followed in abundance by paint, soap, and various chemical containers. Each beach seems to accrue a different type of trash depending on whether the main villains are commercial fishing vessels, naval vessels, smaller recreational fishing boats, or the mighty freighters that ply the Gulf Stream and beyond. On some islands, baseball caps blown off the heads of passengers in speeding skiffs are surprisingly abundant. In this age of souvenir caps, the logos reveal cap origins in a manner not unlike the way heavy minerals in beach sands reveal their source rocks.

Before human beings began contributing substantially to the content of wrack lines, the debris consisted primarily of organic materials. The major constituents were driftwood, seaweed, and especially salt-marsh straw (*Spartina*). Both the driftwood and the salt-marsh straw came from the sound behind the island, carried out to sea through the inlets by tides and winds. These natural wrack lines furnished the organic materials necessary to nourish the start of vegetation growth on newly formed (or newly migrated) islands.

Many different types of seaweed are washed ashore on North Carolina's beaches every summer and left behind in drift lines. Some of these plants originally grew out of the sea floor, while others floated free in the water. Sea lettuce (*Ulva* sp.) is a bright-green seaweed that looks like large, leafy lettuce but feels like waxed paper. Mermaid's hair (*Enteromorpha* sp.) is also bright green but has thin, hairlike stems that grow attached to rocks, shells, or pier pilings. A common type of red seaweed found on our beaches is *Gracilaria*, which usually comes ashore in big tangled piles. These are just a few of the many different kinds of seaweed to be found in drift lines.

But the most common type of seaweed that washes up on our beaches is *Sargassum*, a type of floating algae that forms large lines of seaweed far out at sea, gently carried along by currents. Many juvenile crabs, fish, and sea turtles use the floating *Sargassum* as a source of food, shelter, and protection from predators, and more than twenty different types of seabirds find food in or around the *Sargassum* ecosystem. The Gulf Stream carries large amounts of *Sargassum* off the North Carolina coast, and occasionally storms and waves will bring it ashore. *Sargassum* is brown with leafy branches, and often it has little shells attached. This type of seaweed also has small, berrylike air bladders that act as miniature balloons to keep the plant afloat on the sea surface. When the clumps first wash up on the beach, they are moved to and fro by the swash. Look carefully and you may see a unique *drag mark* in the sand that was produced when the swash moved the seaweed clump over the beach—another riddle of the beach solved. In the drift line itself, you're likely to find many beach critters foraging on this type of vegetation. Perhaps just as important is that these *Sargassum* clumps and other wrack often cause sand to accumulate and thus can be a mechanism by which new dunes begin to form.

Another common drift or wrack line material left on beaches, especially after storms, is *Spartina* straw. *Spartina alterniflora*, the dominant saltwater marsh grass in North Carolina (and along the entire East Coast north of Cape Canaveral), grows in shallow sound waters, mainly on the sound sides of barrier islands. The grasses reach up to three feet in height and seemingly grow as thickly as the turf grass on your lawn. *Spartina* that dies seasonally or is broken up by storms is flushed out to sea through the inlets on outgoing tides. Big storms can leave wrack lines of *Spartina* straw two or three feet thick on the beach (see Fig. 5.2). Seeds of beach grass also find their way into the *Spartina* wrack, which provides a fertile base for these seeds as well as trapping sand that buries the seeds and encourages their germination. A careful look at a wrack line may reveal small green shoots of the first plants to take hold at the back of the beach (either sea oats or American beach grass).

Mud balls are another poststorm debris component. These globs of clay or mud erode out of the highly compacted underlying marsh sediments that crop out on some beaches or migrating barrier islands (Fig. 5.3). The mud balls are rounded by the waves and roll up onto the beach during big storms. Sometimes mud balls can be covered with a layer of shell fragments or sand that accumulated on the outside of the clay as it rolled around with the waves, producing an *armored mud ball.*

Some beach nourishment projects also bring mud balls up to the beach, as happened on Kure and Carolina Beaches in a 1997–98 project. The dredges that pump sand from offshore suck up rocks or chunks of clay sediment from the sea floor along with the sand.

Tar balls also occasionally wash up on our beaches. These sometimes soft, sometimes hard rounded tar masses result from oil spills, large and small. The older the spill, the harder the ball. The volatile components have evaporated away, leaving only viscous tar. Children seem to have a special skill at finding tar balls, stepping on them and then transferring the material to beach cottage interiors!

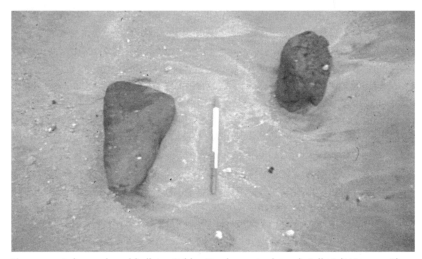

Figure 5.3. Ephemeral mud balls on Holden Beach near Lockwoods Folly Inlet in 1999. These are chunks of well-compacted mud that have broken off an outcrop on the beach and have been rolled about in wave swash to become rounded. These are natural mud balls. Today unnatural mud balls can be a common feature of nourished beaches. Pen for scale.

Air in the Beach

The movement of the tides up and down the beach every half-day or so is a highly visible process carefully watched by fishers, beach buggy enthusiasts, and joggers alike. While these obvious changes are occurring on the beach, important but much less discernible things are happening beneath the surface. As the tide goes out, air replaces water between the sand grains. As the tide comes up, water replaces air. The beach acts like a giant bellows, alternately taking in and expelling air. As the air passes through the sand, many varied features form within the sand as well as on the surface of the beach.

You can watch for yourself as air is forced out of the beach. The best time and place to see this is at mid-to-upper incoming tide levels on the upper beach near the high-tide line. If conditions are right, streams of bubbles will be visible through the thin water film of the uppermost wave swash, especially as the swash begins its return to the sea.

Holes, Rings, Blisters, Pits, and Volcanoes

The expelled air forming the visible bubble trains in the swash usually is emitted from cylindrical, tubelike holes of variable sizes, none larger than the diameter of a large household nail (Fig. 5.4). Our informal term for these, naturally, is *nail holes*. If you count them you will find that they occur in densities of five to one hundred holes per square foot. Their distribution is patchy—many here and none over there—for no obvious reason (a mystery to be solved?). We have talked with many people we meet on the beach about these holes, and almost without exception they assume that the funnels are critter holes. Indeed we have seen sand fleas jump into the holes, but we believe their origin is related to air rather than animals.

When the tide has left the bubble area high and dry, a careful look (on hands and knees) will reveal that some of the nail holes resemble tiny volcanic cones. Inspired by a magnifying glass and our imaginations, we call these features *volcanoes*. The uppermost part of the hole flares out and is rimmed by a tiny, circular mound of sand (Fig. 5.5). The flow of air through the holes was strong enough to remove some sand at the surface and pile it around the rim. Again, if you are watching the swash zone at the right time you can see the tiny eruptions from the holes that expel water and the sand that produces the rim. Figure 5.6 contrasts the beach appearance of a volcano, a pit, and a nail hole.

Sometimes the uppermost layers of the beach resist the breakthrough of the escaping air. Instead of forming a hole to release the air, the sand is forced up into a mound or *blister*, perhaps an inch or two in diameter and extending a fraction of an inch above the beach surface (Fig. 5.7). Careful dissection of blisters with a pocketknife reveals a small, dome-shaped pocket of air above a nail hole, much like an air pocket in a soufflé. Both blisters and volcanoes seem to occur in lower densities than nail holes, averaging one to five per square foot. Blisters, volcanoes, and nail holes often form at the same time and place. The reason a blister sometimes forms, rather than a simple hole, is that the uppermost layers of sand may be slightly consolidated or very lightly cemented by an organic film. The cementation may be due to microscopic salt crystals that have precipitated out of saltwater in the pores between the sand grains. This cement is called

Figure 5.4. Nail holes and small pits, a common beach sight all over the world. These are found most easily on a rising tide above the swash zone. Pits are the holes surrounded by small depressions. As is usually the case, the nail holes in this photo far outnumber the pits. A beach with so many holes is usually one that has recently accreted (built up), and the bubbles occur in the "new" sand.

salcrete, and one can often see it or feel it with bare feet on the uppermost beach, usually above the high-tide line.

After a blister forms, a subsequent wave swash may rush up the beach and decapitate or breach the structure. If a heavy mineral layer was incorporated in the former blister top, a black *ring* forms on the beach (Plate 4, Fig. 5.8). Until we observed how these rings formed, they posed a major riddle for us and were the topic of many discussions and arguments held on the beach. Sometimes removal of a blister by the next swash leaves behind a small, circular depression or *pit* that is larger than a volcano and lacks the characteristic volcanic rim (see Figs. 5.5 and 5.6).

Holes, blisters, rings, and pits sometimes form in distinct lines. Commonly the line appears as the wave swash covers the track left on the beach by a vehicle. As the swash tumbles into the tire depression, air is forced out of the sand. The air escapes as a spectacular row or chain of bubbles, visible as long as water remains in the old track. Sometimes the swash

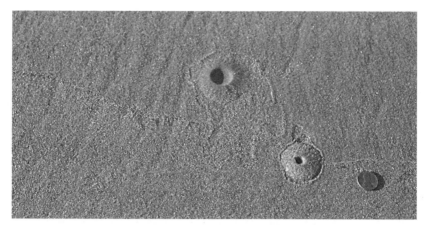

Figure 5.5. Volcanoes on the beach! These features are formed when a relatively large volume of air escapes the beach. Accompanied by water, the escaping air brings with it sand that piles up into a cone. A careful look at this photo reveals at least two faint swash marks and equally faint rhomboid ripple marks. Penny for scale.

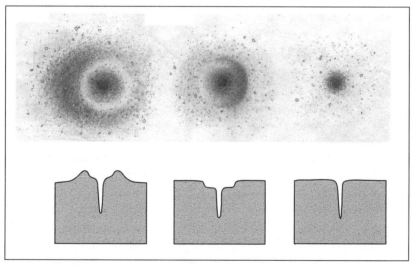

Figure 5.6. Comparison of a volcano, pit, and nail hole on the surface. Some pits and nail holes may be volcanoes truncated by swash erosion, but pits and nail holes also form independently of volcanoes. (Drawing by Charles Pilkey)

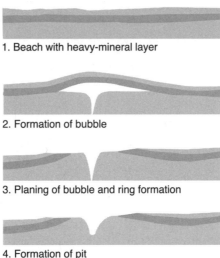

1. Beach with heavy-mineral layer

2. Formation of bubble

3. Planing of bubble and ring formation

4. Formation of pit

Figure 5.7. Idealized cross-sections showing the formation of a blister and its evolution into a ring and a pit. When the domed heavy-mineral layer is truncated by erosion, the visible ring is produced on the beach surface. (Drawing by Charles Pilkey)

removes all evidence of the tire track, and only the line of holes or blisters remains. Even footprints in the sand and pieces of debris will promote the formation of bubbling holes, but they can also be found on smooth beaches without obstructions.

Under the right conditions and with a little practice, it is possible to manufacture your own line of holes on the beach. Take a long piece of driftwood and place it high enough on the beach for the swash to run over it but not move it. You will observe a line of bubbles emanating from the sand as the water cascades over the obstacle.

Sometimes blisters or rings occur in a mysterious, evenly spaced pattern, with each ring a few inches from its neighboring ring on the beach surface (see Plate 4). This rather spectacular arrangement may cover a few square yards of beach above the water line (Fig. 5.9). Our explanation for this incredibly symmetrical pattern is that it forms as air rises through a section of beach that has very uniform-sized sand lacking irregularities like seashells. Another riddle.

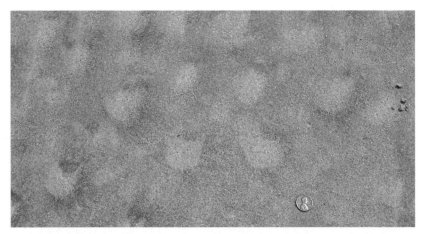

Figure 5.8. Rings on Pea Island, spring 2002. These rings have faded a bit, probably because it has rained since their formation. Faint raindrop imprints are visible in the photo. The regular spacing of the rings is probably due to the escape of air through a very uniform layer of sand. Another riddle in the sand! Penny for scale.

Another important manifestation of air rising through beaches is not visible at the surface. Veteran beach strollers are painfully familiar with the fact that some stretches of beach between the high- and low-tide lines are easier to walk on than others. Why is some sand hard and some soft—so soft that you may sink ankle-deep or more into the sand?

The same mechanism that pumps air into the beach to form holes, blisters, pits, and volcanoes is also responsible for soft sand. Water rising with the tide below the surface of the beach forces air up through the sand. When this air cannot escape rapidly enough, it causes bubbles to form within the uppermost sand layers. Our name for this phenomenon is *bubbly sand*. When you walk across bubbly sand, which may have no surface expression to warn you of its presence, your weight collapses the bubbles. Your feet sink into the sand and suddenly an easy stroll on the beach becomes a more strenuous exercise (Fig. 5.10).

It is easy to see the bubbles in the sand that are causing your footprint to be much larger than it was on nearby hard sand. Force your hand into the sand and bring up a chunk of the beach with a fresh vertical face. Look at this sharp face, and you will see large and small cavities that were formed

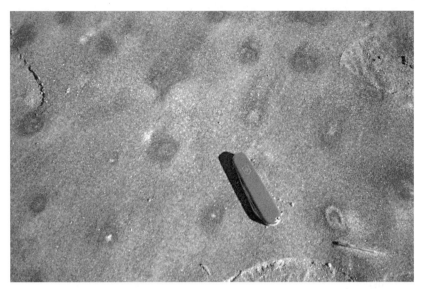

Figure 5.9. Regularly spaced rings on a Bodie Island beach. The actual dark ring is a heavy-mineral layer that was uplifted into a blister and then was truncated by a wave swash. The knife is for scale.

by the air forced into the beach. It may take several tries to perfect the sampling technique, but it works. Breaking the chunk of sand apart sometimes reveals cavities concentrated along the horizontal bedding planes. In these cases, the air was forced into the beach vertically and then flowed horizontally between layers of sand grains of differing sizes (Plate 5).

Soft or bubbly sand typically forms on relatively flat areas of the upper beach when the waves are pushing new sand up onto the beach—for example, when the beach is recovering from a storm. Immediately after a storm, there is usually no soft sand, and beach strolling is much easier. Freshly deposited sand is also more amenable to the formation of blisters and nail holes, relative to a fresh erosion surface.

Bubbly sand must be uniform in grain size and must contain few shell fragments. Finer-grained sand seems to be much more susceptible to bubble formation than coarse sand. This may be because air does not travel as rapidly through a wet, fine sand as it does through a wet, coarse sand. Because sand tends to be finer on southern North Carolina beaches,

Figure 5.10. Footprints in bubbly sand. Whoever walked across this patch of bubbly sand at Mason Inlet suddenly found the going quite tough.

bubbly sand is more common there. So there should arguably be more bubbly sand on Sunset Beach than in Kill Devil Hills.

If you come upon a zone of very soft, water-saturated sand, tap your foot repeatedly on the same spot. By doing so, you may cause the sand to become *quicksand*, or to liquefy. The vibration disturbs the packing of the sand grains and causes air bubbles to collapse; water surrounds the grains, and the sand—at least the upper few inches of it—behaves as a liquid.

Where does all the air in a beach come from? It probably involves several factors, the most important of which is simply the rushing in of air to fill the intergranular cavities left by falling tides. When the tide rises again, the incoming water pushes out the air. But we think that many of the air-formed features on beaches may be responses to processes taking place in the upper few inches of the beach. The formation of bubble lines in tire tracks and on the landward side of obstacles on the beach are indications of the shallow genesis of these features.

Sam Smith, an observant Australian coastal engineer, offers another explanation. He notes that, as waves finally break up into a sheet of swash, surging up a beach, the thin layer of swash water is divided up into a number of cells (Fig. 5.11). Smith refers to the cells as *swash footballs*, which more or less describes the shape of each cell when viewed from above. The best way to see swash footballs is to visit a North Carolina fishing pier and walk out to a position just over the swash zone. Look for patterns like the one shown in Figure 5.11, although it is important to note that they are not always there.

Each of these cells is a separate wave orbital that, at its front end, captures air and forces it into the sediment. At the back or seaward end, air is sucked out of the sand. Swash after swash pumps air into the sand, creating ever more bubbles and air holes in the sand and perhaps expanding some holes that are already there. The process is poorly understood, and it is not absolutely certain that it is of consequence in the formation of nail holes and blisters. This is a riddle that someone (not necessarily a scientist) might solve by standing in the swash zone for many hours.

Foam, Swash, Imprints:
How Currents and Winds Sculpt the Surface

The surface of the beach is like a canvas painted in diverse patterns. Each pattern reflects a difference in the manner in which currents, waves and winds, and organisms operate on the beach. These *bedforms*—a general term for all small-scale features on the surface of the beach—result from a huge number of physical processes acting in combination. Each type of bedform provides clues to the processes that created it, but just as in the case of features formed by air moving through the beach, we still have a lot to learn about all of them.

Swash marks, one of the more prevalent bedforms, are minute ridges of sand or debris left behind by the most landward reach of an individual wave swash (Fig. 5.12). At low tide, the entire beach may be covered by

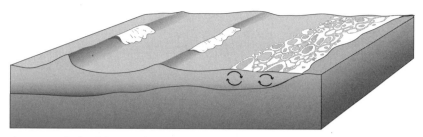

Figure 5.11. Idealized diagram, both cross-section and overhead view, of the swash zone foot-balls and the wave orbitals associated with them. These orbitals may constitute one of the methods by which air is forced into or out of the beach. (Drawing by Charles Pilkey)

these long wavy lines running more or less parallel to the water line, each one a trace of the single wave that created it. The swash mark is like a microscopic wrack line.

One component of some swash lines is floating sand. As we can some-times see with careful observation, the surface tension of the water allows sand to float, and the grains can end up on the advancing edge of the swash. When this water soaks into the beach, some of the floating sand carried along the leading edge settles to form the swash mark. The slight difference in grain size and composition between the floaters and the regu-lar beach sand is one reason that swash marks stand out in relief.

The swash commonly aligns the surface sand grains as it washes over the beach face, leaving streaks of various kinds that reflect the up-and-down motion of the swash. This pattern, which may consist of faint ir-regularities, streaks, or microridges and grooves up and down the beach or perpendicular to swash marks, is called *parting lineation.*

Sea foam is responsible for one of the more puzzling riddles of the sand, especially if one comes upon it hours after a storm has dissipated and the foam is gone. This foam forms naturally as pounding storm waves churn up sea-floor sediments. The process extracts organic matter from the sedi-ment and violently churns it all up into the white, bubbly mass known as sea foam, which looks as though someone has poured bubble bath into the waves. Often inorganic clay particles (mud) are attached to the bubbles, so when the foam bubbles eventually collapse, a thin film of gray-colored

5.12. Swash lines along with a tire track extending far down the beach. Each line represents the furthest incursion of wave swash upon the beach during a falling tide.

mud is left behind on the upper beach or wherever the foam comes to rest. Those who have waded through a pile of foam have noticed that same gray film clinging to their clothes.

Sometimes after a big storm the foam can accumulate to a thickness of several feet where the shoreline is backed by a vertical dune scarp or some other obstacle (Fig. 5.13). We have walked into piles four feet thick against a dune scarp at Nags Head. If there is no obstacle to prevent the foam from blowing ashore, it will accumulate up against buildings or on nearby streets. At the height of a storm, it is common to see flying clumps of foam.

During fairweather conditions, small amounts of foam are commonly visible in the surf, where the waves are breaking, and the swash zone, where the waves are washing up on the beach (Fig. 5.14). A distinct foam swash line remains behind. As clumps of foam are carried or rolled up the

Figure 5.13. Foam on the upper beach at Nags Head during a nor'easter in February 1998. If the storm persists long enough and if the winds are onshore, the foam will pile up into thicknesses of several feet against the dune scarp. Note the large dune erosion scarp and the fragments of dune walkovers in the surf zone.

beach, they leave a very fine track across the sand, equal in width to the diameter of the clump. Typically, *foam stripes* run in parallel tracks in the direction of the wind, leaving a distinct pattern on the beach. Clumps of foam may also be carried across the beach by the wind in a hop, skip, and jump fashion, leaving intermittent traces or *foam tracks* where the clump touches down on the beach (Fig 5.15). Where a patch of foam comes to rest, a final set of bubble impressions may be left in the surface of the sand. All of these features are very fine and difficult to see. They are best observed as they are forming, but once you've seen them form you will be able to find such traces well after the foam has disappeared.

A less puzzling texture found on beaches is *raindrop imprints* (Fig. 5.16). The impact of raindrops during a heavy rain will indent the sand surface. As the rain soaks into the sand, a textured surface marked by irregular pits is left behind. These imprints are easily washed away by the

Figure 5.14. Patches of foam on a stormy Bogue Banks beach in the spring of 2002. Foam is created by organic matter stored in bottom sediments and later stirred up by storm waves. Foam may accumulate in piles that are several feet thick when it is blown up against some obstacle such as a dune erosion scarp.

next high tide or disruptions to the beach such as vehicular traffic or dry winds, so they usually don't last long. By contrast, raindrop impressions on the surface of bare dunes may persist for days. Raindrop imprints have even been found in many ancient sandstones, some of them millions of years old, so under the right conditions "permanent" preservation of these ephemeral features can occur.

Ripple marks are one of the most common bedforms found in the intertidal zone of the beach (Plate 6). They are also a very common feature in ancient rocks.

Ripple marks form any place where there are the right kind of winds, waves, and currents—on dunes, on the beach, on the shoreface, or way offshore on the continental shelf. In fact, they can form anywhere in the oceans. These low ridges of sand line up in a repetitive pattern perpendicular to the direction of the water current or wind that created them. They look like miniature dunes and can cover very large areas. Ripple marks are formed by wind or water passing over the surface at a high

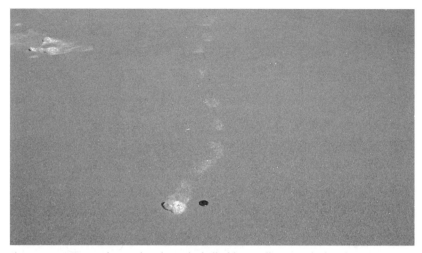

Figure 5.15. Foam tracks on a beach. As the ball of foam rolls across the beach in response to the wind, it leaves a faint mark in the sand each time it comes to rest. During waning storm conditions, when large volumes of foam may be produced, the surface of large areas of the beach will bear the marks of rolling foam balls. Penny for scale.

enough velocity to move sand. Because ripple marks are found in ancient rocks, they have been studied in detail over the years in the hope that they might help to determine the geologic history of rocks. In this chapter we'll only scratch the surface of ripple marks.

Of the numerous varieties of ripple marks that exist, North Carolina beaches most frequently have both long-crested or *wave ripples* and irregular short-crested or *current ripples.*

Although wave ripples can be nearly symmetric, the fact that waves are directional means the ripples are moving forward, so usually they are slightly asymmetric in cross-section. Each individual ripple is like a wave in its geometry, possessing a crest and trough. The crests of adjacent ripples may be either straight or gently curved (sinuous), but they are semiparallel, and one side of the ripple slopes gently while the other side is steep. The steep side faces in the direction that the current is moving. To observe this asymmetry, you may have to get down close to the beach surface or look at the beach from different angles to catch the light-and-

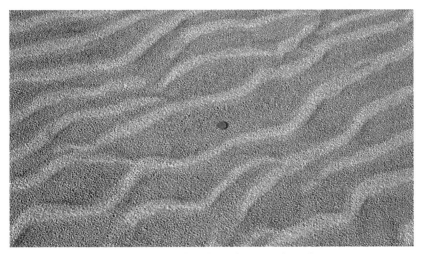

Figure 5.16. Raindrop imprints on top of ripple marks. Penny for scale.

shadow effect. In some wave ripple sets, the parallel crests occasionally converge to form zigzag junctures.

Wave ripples are forming somewhere in the nearshore most of the time, on both the rising and the falling tides. As conditions change, a newly formed set of ripples may be washed out, only to reform again on the next tidal cycle. Sometimes a well-formed set of ripples will be modified without being destroyed as new wave dynamics take over, resulting in a variety of ripple forms including *flat-topped ripples* (Figs. 5.17 and 5.18), in which the ripple crests are truncated by erosive conditions; *interference ripples* that form when waves come from different directions during the formation of the ripples, as in areas where sandbars create different wave-refraction patterns; and *ladder-back ripples* (Fig 5.19), in which a slightly younger set of ripples forms atop or across a pre-existing set of ripple marks, as on tidal flats during rising and falling tides. *Flaser ripples* (Fig. 5.20) have mud in the troughs between the ripple crests, a phenomenon that reflects a calming down of conditions leading ultimately to still water in which mud is deposited.

Where water flows as a current in a channel such as a trough or runnel, current ripples form. These ripples are usually much more asymmetric in

Figure 5.17. Flat-topped ripple marks that have flattened to the point that the original ripples are almost destroyed. This ripple geometry was created during a tidal cycle in which the ripples first formed when the current was flowing to the right, then on the falling tide the ripples were decapitated as the sediment was carried back to the left.

Figure 5.18. Flat-topped ripple marks from a sand flat on the lagoon side of Shackleford Banks. These occur when the wave conditions favorable for ripple mark formation change to conditions favorable for ripple mark destruction. The latter change in conditions came about as the tide went out, eroding the tops of the ripples before their exposure. See camera lens cap for scale.

Figure 5.19. Ladder-back ripples indicating waves and/or currents coming from two different directions, or possibly a younger set of ripple marks forming atop a pre-existing ripple set. (Duncan Heron Photography)

Figure 5.20. Flaser ripples created by Hurricane Bertha on Topsail Island in July 1996. These lunate-shaped ripples have mud in their troughs, an indication that during the storm conditions progressed from strong wave activity to very calm seas that allowed the mud to settle out. See wallet for scale.

cross-section than wave-formed ripples, and their crests are less continuous and not necessarily parallel to the crests of adjacent ripples. When you look down on them, the shapes of the ripples can show a variety of forms, and typically these shapes are used to describe the ripples. For example, groups of ripples or ripple trains may be described as *linguoid, cuspate, lunate,* or *catenary.*

A good place in which to watch ripple marks form and still keep your feet dry is a trough on the beach (the backside of a berm) that is still filled with water on the ebbing tide. As the tide continues to fall, the trough will drain, and even though the water is only a few inches deep, a moderately swift flow will begin to move the sand grains, shaping the trough floor into a field of current ripple marks. The sand grains move up the gentle backside of the ripple and either jet off the crest or fall into the trough of the ripple's leading edge. The ripple then migrates downstream. In some instances, dark heavy-mineral grains or coarser shell particles will selectively accumulate in the ripple troughs, making the shape of the structure more apparent.

Another ripple form that develops on the falling tide is the *antidune* (Fig. 5.21). The name derives from the fact that the steep face looks upstream, just the opposite of most ripples and dunes. This reversed orientation develops when backwash flows rapidly down the beach and a gentle wavelike bedform develops in phase with the water surface. Watch the backwash after a wave breaks, and for a brief instant this surface is visible although the ripple bedform is not. As the tide continues to fall, however, this part of the beach emerges, and wide stripes appear on the beach marking the positions of antidune bedforms. Dark heavy minerals are often preferentially concentrated in troughs, enhancing the appearance of the stripes.

Ripples can also be found on the upper beach, above the high-tide swash mark, and in the dunes, where wind is the driving force behind moving the sand. Like the long-crested wave-formed ripples, *wind ripple marks* (Fig. 5.22) on sand dunes are rhythmic, long crested, and asymmetric in cross-section. They line up parallel to one another, perpendicular to the direction of the latest winds, with the steep face in the direction of that latest wind. Wind direction may change several times a day, so wind-ripple orientations will change as well, and quickly. Typically, the troughs

Figure 5.21. Antidune bedform on the lower beach formed as the tide was going out. The steep face of these features looks upstream, the opposite of most ripples. The ripples are spaced about a foot apart in this photo.

of wind ripples are shallower than those of wave ripples, and as a result it may be difficult to distinguish their asymmetry. Again, dark heavy-mineral concentrations in the troughs may produce visible stripes that make ripple shape more apparent. These dark-colored heavy minerals are concentrated as the wind selectively transports the lighter-density minerals faster than the heavy ones.

In addition to ripples, the wind leaves other surface markings on beaches and dunes. As noted earlier, when foam is blown across the beach a bubble track or foam stripe results. If an object is dragged over the surface by swash or wind, a drag mark results. The object being moved is referred to as a *tool*, and a variety of puzzling patterns can develop depending on the type of tool. In the dunes, the tip ends of grass fronds, plant leaves, and exposed rootlets etch curious, featherlike patterns on the surface of the sand when the plant is blown about. These plant scratchings often form a distinctive arc-shaped ring or *plant arc* (Fig. 5.23) or scribe mark.

Figure 5.22. Wind-ripple marks on a dune on Shackleford Banks, formed by a wind that moved from right to left in the photo. Wind-ripple marks rapidly change their orientation as winds change directions. (Duncan Heron Photography)

Adhesion ripples and related adhesion structures are another set of wind-developed bedforms. Sand blowing over a wet surface will begin to stick or adhere to that surface. Capillary action continues to move water up between the grains, and more windblown sand sticks to the surface. The resulting adhesion surface may have an irregular ripple form or a scabby or wartlike pattern (Fig 5.24). Often these surfaces develop adjacent to the trough (runnel) on the beach at low tide. The surface is wet as water drains out of the beach and traps sand being moved over the beach by the wind.

Rhomboid ripple marks are a special kind of beach bedform (Figs. 5.25 and 5.26). These V-shaped features form as wave swash goes back and forth in a receding tide. The Vs always point toward the land. The pattern may also be produced by backwash around objects on the beach such as shells.

Patterns on the beach often are generated where even the smallest obstruction interferes with water or wind current flow. Pebbles and larger shells cause the flow around them to scour the sand, creating *crescent*

Figure 5.23. Arc-shaped tracings in dune sand on Ocracoke Island, formed by dune grass moving in the wind. Most of the arcs have been somewhat obscured by raindrop imprints.

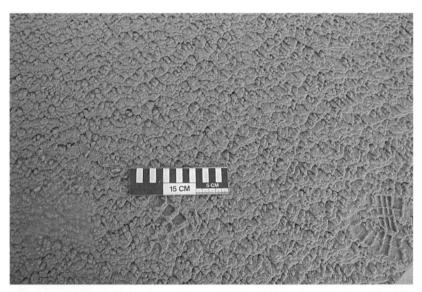

Figure 5.24. Adhesion ripples form as dry sand is blown over very wet sand, creating this strange, knobby surface.

Figure 5.25. Rhomboid ripple marks from the intertidal zone at Hammocks Beach State Park.

Figure 5.26. Rhomboid ripple marks. These marks can be seen in the intertidal zone on relatively steep beach surfaces. They are formed by the wave swash. The tips of the angles that constitute the ripple marks always point up the beach slope.

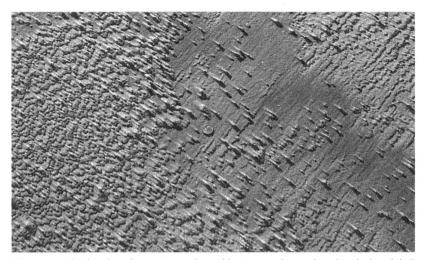

Figure 5.27. This beach surface texture is formed by tiny windrows of sand in the lee of shell fragments and other coarse particles. It sometimes occurs when the surface of the beach is lightly cemented by salt evaporated from seawater (salcrete). No question which way the wind that created this surface was blowing! Penny for scale.

marks. Where the wind blows over such coarse particles, tiny windrows of sand build up behind each shell or pebble, giving a strong directional texture to the beach that may change as wind direction changes (Fig. 5.27). Similar but larger-scale windrows of sand develop on a shelly beach like Shackleford Banks when strong winds blow in a consistent direction, creating strongly parallel sand rows oriented downwind of each shell.

Within a short distance across the beach-dune system, you will often see several different fields of ripple marks. With a little practice you will soon be able to recognize them as signatures of different sets of wave, water, and wind current processes. The best way to understand ripples is to observe them yourself on the beach you know best. Note what kind of ripples form when the wind blows toward the land, when the wave swash is small and when it is large, and the differences that develop between wet and dry sand. The observant beach reader, with enough experience, can make sense of the riddle of ripple marks. You can become the world's leading expert for your beach.

Wind: The Modifier

As noted, some features on the beach owe their origins in part to the wind (the orientation of foam stripes, adhesion ripples), and wind-produced bedforms become dominant on the dry beach and into the dunes. Wind ripple marks, shell lag pavement, and crossbedding (see Chapter 3) are good examples. As the wind scours the laminated sands of the backbeach, the differential downcutting produces intriguing patterns, both horizontally and vertically. On the surface, differential exposure of the layers of light-colored sand and black heavy-mineral sand creates contrasting contoured stripes (see Fig. 2.7). As sand is blown out (deflated) by the wind, vertical faces are etched to reveal the laminae of varied color and grain size. If a resistant object such as a clump of seaweed or a shell holds the underlying sand in place, a *pedestal* will result. These columns resemble tiny buttes or sometimes mushrooms (Fig. 5.28). Look for them on sand flats on a windy day.

Your quest to understand sedimentary structures will take you from the beach into the dunes. There you will see wind ripples, windrows of sand in the shadow of plants and debris (see Plate 3), crescent scouring around wind obstacles, plant arcs scribed by grass fronds and exposed rootlets, and pitted surfaces due to raindrop impressions. But there is much more to discover: the footprints of birds, rabbits, raccoons, and other animals; tracks and traces that range in size from those of insects to those of snakes; strange little ridges produced by insects that burrow horizontally just below the surface; and the holes produced by various burrowers including bees (be careful). You may find the ingenious pit-trap of an ant lion (Fig. 5.29) or the intricate patterns produced by the eroded edges of crossbeds. The dunes also pose riddles.

Singing Sand

The sounds of nature associated with a day at the beach may include the splash of waves lapping or crashing onto the shore, the cry of scavenging seagulls, or the keening of a stiff wind blowing past your ears. Walking along the beach may produce a new sound, one that comes from the sand

Figure 5.28. Pedestal structures produced by wind erosion on the beach at Cape Lookout. *Top*: These sand ""mushrooms" form when the upper sand layer is more resistant because of moisture content or cementation (salcrete). *Bottom*: A closeup of the center sand mushroom shows the grain size variation in the laminae. These delicate features are found on the sandy flats of the upper beach. (Ken Sussman Photography; furnished by the U.S. National Park Service)

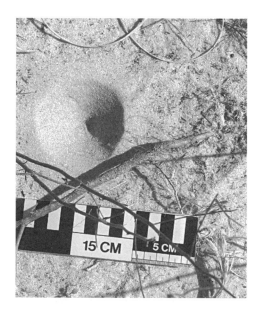

Figure 5.29. Ant lion pit in the dunes at Fort Macon State Park on Bogue Banks. The steep slope of the pit collapses when the prey ventures into the pit, carrying lunch to the "lion."

itself. As you tromp along, the sand may sing, bark, or squeak at you! It all depends on how you choose to describe the sound.

Singing or barking occurs on most sand beaches of the world. It goes by a lot of other names, including musical sand, whistling sand, squeaking sand, and, in Japan, frog-sound sand. Whatever its name, the noise is produced when you scuff your feet on certain patches of sand on the upper beach. Sand deposited both by water and by wind may bark or sing.

In order for the sand to sing, all of the grains must be of similar size (that is, they must be well sorted). Singing sand usually has grains that are close to spherical in shape and have dust-free surfaces. The sand must also be pollution-free. That is, there must be no organic matter between or on the grains.

The sound is produced by the shear that occurs when one layer of sand grains slides over the layer beneath it, with all the grains moving in unison. When there is dust or some kind of pollution on the sand grains, the friction between layers is reduced and the sand is silent.

Not all sands bark alike. The sounds have a large frequency range, and the frequency is different for each patch of singing or barking sand. Fine sands (individual grains barely visible to the naked eye) produce only a poor, weak-sounding bark. Medium-sized sands can emit a range of sounds, from a faint squeak to a high-pitched yelp. The best and loudest barks come from medium-sized sand grains like those on beaches between Cape Hatteras and Cape Lookout.

Water also plays a role in the ability of sand grains to produce sound. Although water will usually silence singing sands by causing the grains to stick together instead of shearing past each other, adding small amounts of water to the sand can actually raise the pitch of the squeaking sound. Thus, though sand sings primarily on the dry upper beach above the normal high-tide line, some sands have been reported to sing on the lower beach near the low-tide line. One theory holds that sand may produce sounds under water when waves crash on the bottom under just the right circumstances (whatever these may be), but no one has reported the phenomenon for North Carolina beaches.

A cousin to singing sand is booming sand, produced as sand slides down the face of large dunes. Booming is primarily a desert phenomenon, but coastal dunes occasionally produce the noise under dry conditions. It is said to be a low-frequency roar or groan that can be quite startling, especially at night. Descriptions of booming sand from historical records are surprisingly common. In ninth-century China, groups of people slid down the Mount Ming-sha-shan sand dunes to announce with thundering sounds the arrival of a boy's festival day. And in Hawaii, people attributed a religious cause to the phenomenon, believing that the booming dunes of Kauai were the sounds of disgruntled spirits.

Shipwrecks on the Beach

The artifacts of human interactions with the sea are another beach component that reflects the past history of people and storms. Very old structures or their ruins, such as lighthouses (Cape Hatteras), gun emplacements (Cape Lookout and Bogue Banks), and fortifications (Fort Fisher) provide reference points for earlier shoreline positions. But the most fascinating markers of past history are shipwrecks.

In the late 1800s, the coastguardsmen of the lifesaving station on Parramore Island, Virginia, woke up to find the hulk of a wooden sailing vessel on the beach right in front of their station house. At first the shocked coastguardsmen thought a wreck had occurred, unbeknownst to them, during the previous night's storm. But a closer examination of the wreck revealed that it was a guano-carrying ship that had sunk with the loss of all hands some fourteen years earlier. Hull timbers of this ship are still visible on the beach at Parramore Island.

In 1972, after a moderate storm, a large pile of wooden ship debris suddenly appeared on the beach at Core Banks, North Carolina. The debris included the block and tackle from the ship's rigging, the ship's steering wheel, oak keel timbers, and cypress planks covered with thin sheets of copper. Local scavengers quickly made off with much of the remains. The name of the wreck remains unknown, but a Smithsonian shipwreck expert believed that it was a type of vessel manufactured as late as 1840. It may have sailed the seas as recently as the first decade of the twentieth century, or it may have been a Confederate blockade-runner.

Beachcombers who walk the beaches of the Outer Banks, especially during the winter, frequently come across small—and sometimes large—timbers from shipwrecks. The National Park Service does not allow such artifacts to be removed from the National Seashores, but if you should discover part of an old shipwreck, contact the Park Service office. Once removed from the water, the timbers, especially those made of oak, quickly deteriorate unless costly measures are taken to protect them. Cypress timbers seem to be much more hardy.

The mystery of these beached shipwrecks is that they usually arrive on the beach in good condition. Few show signs of attached barnacles, mussels, or seaweed, or the effects of burrowing worms; there is no evidence of the timbers being worn by rolling around on the bottom of the sea for years, either. Clearly these remains did not lie exposed on the sea floor for any length of time. Most likely the vessels were buried in sand before being unearthed and washed ashore. In Texas, a whole shrimp trawler was once found buried in a beach, with only the tip of its mast protruding.

Liquefaction of the sea floor could be responsible for the initial burial of shipwreck debris, which likely occurs under the pounding of storm waves. As the waves penetrate the sand on the sea floor, they may temporarily turn it into quicksand. This liquefaction has to occur where there are relatively thick deposits of sand on the continental shelf. Any ship's timbers that sank while the sea floor was very briefly in this quicksand state would be buried and thereby preserved from the ravages of sea-floor organisms. Future storms might then expose and push the wreckage ashore. The last voyage of the wreck is to sail ashore via the sea floor. In many places offshore of North Carolina beaches, especially between Cape Lookout and Cape Fear, widespread rock outcrops prevent the buildup of sand sufficient to enclose a wreck.

Connections: The Ocean, the Beach, Life

Ripple marks, bubble holes, heavy-mineral placers, sand texture, each tells a story of processes shaping sediment—the endless renewal that is the beach. A swash line is the last clue left by the edge of a small dying wave, but its erasure provides the grains that will become part of the next swash. On a grander scale, the regional storm changing the shape of your beach at its apex will leave a drift line of wrack as its local record of an event that links this beach to many beaches. Events that appear to be of little consequence hold the beginnings of other beach events. In the case of the wrack line, another link in the chain of beach life and the associated sand is connected. The wrack line provides a basis for a microecosystem, has the potential to trap sand and initiate dune growth, and contains the seeds of life that may populate sand dunes and build up barrier islands.

Perhaps you have noted, in our descriptions of bubbly sand, singing sand, holes, and blisters, that we do not always know how a particular structure forms or what creates a particular phenomenon. You might be able to solve some of these riddles of the beach by being observant and watching the different features that form under various wave, wind, and tide conditions. Keep in mind that all beaches are different, and the answer to a puzzle on Wrightsville Beach may not hold true for the beach in Currituck.

six

Life Signs: Beach Critters, Past and Present

Most beachcombers carry a bird book or shell book with them on their walks, or at least they have one on the shelf back in the cottage to help them identify their sightings or finds of the day. Among the many things you might find on your beach stroll are an array of colorfully named clams and snails (turkey wings, whelks, olives, baby's ears, or the elusive Scotch Bonnet), though only a few species of clams and crustaceans actually live in the beach. You also may find shell fragments that did not come from either snails or clams; the most common are barnacle plates which are difficult to distinguish from clams at first glance. This chapter considers these creatures from a different perspective than the standard seashell identification book. For example, most people are surprised to learn that by far the majority of shells that they have picked up on North Carolina beaches and identified in their shell guide are, in fact, fossils.

Even long-dead animals leave important signs in and on the beach, and the calcareous (calcium carbonate) shells of the organisms are a source of future sand grains. The color of these grains reveals their history of burial or exposure on the beach. Each species may tell us something about barrier island history, and shell orientation on the beach surface may reflect previous wave and current conditions. And the organisms may be sensitive indicators of pollution or artificial beach nourishment. They offer us clues that might enable us to unlock additional riddles of the sand.

From Shells to Sand: The Carbonate Fraction

Not all of the sand beneath your feet came from the rivers of the Piedmont. In North Carolina, anywhere from 1 to 50 percent of beach and dune material can consist of calcium carbonate ($CaCO_3$), the carbonate fractions of both beach and dune sands. In general, dune sand tends to be less calcareous (5 percent or less of $CaCO_3$) than beach sand (typically 10 percent or less). The carbonate fraction in both beaches and dunes is derived from once-living shelled organisms (Table 6.1). But most of the "living" organisms in beach and dune sands died long ago, and most of the shells on North Carolina's beaches are fossils, hundreds to thousands of years old.

Calcium carbonate can occur in two different mineral forms, *aragonite* and *calcite*. The chemical composition of the two is identical, but the crystalline structure (arrangement of the atoms) is different. The dominant carbonate mineral in the beaches of North Carolina is aragonite, which is found in fossil snail and clam shells as well as in some corals. The shells of oysters and a few other species are made up of the mineral calcite. Sea urchins and sand dollars are composed of a form of calcite called *high-magnesium calcite*, but the shells of these organisms are rarely found whole on beaches because they are quite fragile and disintegrate easily in breaking waves. You are most likely to find the shells of sand dollars and sea urchins on lagoon beaches, where waves are lower and don't break the shells into pieces as quickly as the waves on the open ocean side.

After animals die, their shells may end up on the beach in several ways. Only a minority of the shells on a North Carolina beach are from animals that died in recent years. Most are much older—often thousands of years old—and they arrived on the beaches as the barrier islands migrated over the old lagoon sands that were once located behind the islands. When the shells popped out on the open ocean shoreface, they were eventually pushed up onto the beach by fairweather waves. A few shells on the beach come from animals that originally lived near the beach during a time of lower sea level, and these, too, eventually were moved to the present beach by waves.

Years ago, using the radiocarbon-dating technique, we determined the age of the composite carbonate fraction from a large beach sample taken from Shackleford Banks. It proved to be between seven thousand and nine thousand years old. Many more dates are needed to be certain, but most likely the composite shell fraction of most North Carolina beaches will be thousands of years old.

Table 6.1. Common Shells Found on North Carolina Beaches

BIVALVES (CLAMS)	GASTROPODS (SNAILS)	OTHER ORGANISMS
Angel wings	Auger shells	Barnacles
Ark shells	Keyhole limpets	Corals
Cockles	Moon shells	Jellyfish
Coquina clams	Olive shells	Sand dollars
Cross-barred Venus clams	Oyster drills	Sea urchin tests
Disk shells	Scotch bonnets	Sharks' teeth
Jingle shells	Slipper shells	Skate egg casings
Kitten's paw shells	Sundials	Starfish (sea star)
Oysters	Tulip shells	Whelk egg casings
Quahogs (clams)	Whelks	
Pen shells	(lightning, knobbed,	
Razor clams	channeled)	
Scallops	Worm shells	
Surf clams		
Turkey wings		

Note: Bivalves are mollusks, having two shells that are usually symmetrical. Gastropods (snails) are also mollusks, but they have only one shell, usually coiled. When the animal withdraws into its shell, the opening is closed by a second, shelly, hard part, the operculum. These thin, calcareous opercula are not uncommon but may go unrecognized by shell collectors.

In recent years, some shells have been found on North Carolina beaches (near Buxton and on Shackleford Banks and Core Banks) that are forty thousand years old. The shells were too old to date by the radiocarbon method; instead, their ages were determined using a special technique known as amino acid dating. A number of the state's beaches can no longer be dated for the purpose of determining island geologic history because beachfill projects have dumped shelly sands from other places on top of the native beach sands.

On many beaches, the most common—and easiest to find—fossil shell is the oyster (*Crassostrea virginica*). Oysters live on the island backsides or in lagoons, not the front or open ocean side of islands. Thus all oysters on North Carolina ocean beaches are "out-of-place" fossils (unless they are the remnants of an oyster roast).

Occasionally, one can find shells of extinct creatures that lived millions of years ago. By far the most spectacular of these are the giant oysters (*Crassostrea gigantisima*) sometimes thrown up on North Topsail Beach and Onslow Beach after storms. These shells, up to three times the size of the largest modern oysters, would have made some meal! They are perhaps twenty million years old (Miocene period) in age and have been eroded out of a slowly deteriorating limestone outcrop a few hundred yards offshore. Divers have observed that the sea floor there is littered with these giant fossil oyster shells.

Shells in the surf zone will slowly break apart after tumbling around in the waves and swash. Eventually they are broken into smaller and smaller fragments until finally they are reduced to sand-sized grains. The process is helped along by skates and rays, which crunch the shells of the organisms they eat. A concentrated mix of ground-up and rounded shells is called *shell hash*, which sometimes covers large areas of the beach (Fig. 6.1), especially on the Outer Banks. The rate at which the shells break apart and the degree of breakup depends in part on the wave energy of that particular beach. For instance, on the Outer Banks, shells are usually smoother and more rounded than those on Sunset Beach, where the wave energy, or average wave height, is significantly lower.

It takes years for the shell material to be worn down into sand-sized grains. In the earlier stages of the physical weathering (breaking apart) process, shell edges become rounded and smooth (see Fig. 6.1). On the Outer Banks, these very rounded shells can be found in stores, where they are sometimes sold as jewelry. The more rounded a shell is, the more time it has spent tumbling around in the waves. Some, such as the pen shell and the jingle shell, are too fragile to last long and break quickly into microscopic fragments instead of rounding and polishing over time.

Artificial beachfill in so-called nourished beaches consists of sand and shells brought in from nearby locations, such as inlets, lagoons, or the continental shelf. This addition often changes the entire composition of shell

Figure 6.1. Shell hash is composed of shell fragments that have been rounded and polished by the waves and sand. These shells reflect a long period of abrasion in the surf zone of the high-wave beach at Buxton. Paperclips for scale.

species on the beach, and the natural characteristics of some North Carolina beaches no longer remain intact (Atlantic Beach, Pine Knoll Shores, Indian Beach, Emerald Isle, Figure Eight Island, Wrightsville Beach, Carolina Beach, Kure Beach, Oak Island, Ocean Isle Beach). Places that allow four-wheel drive vehicles on the beach, such as Ocracoke and parts of Bogue Banks, often have highly irregular, gravel-sized shells, which have been crushed as the cars or trucks drive over them (Fig. 6.2). In fact, vehicles break up beach shells much more efficiently than waves. On Topsail Island, at any time of year, you are likely to find bulldozers scraping sand from the beach to form "dunes." You can guess what bulldozers do to shells!

During a 2002 beach nourishment project in Pine Knoll Shores, dredgers used a technique that broke up most of the shells. In addition, the beachfill (beach nourishment) source area was the nearby shoreface, which was much shellier than the original beach. The result is a beach that is too shelly and sharp for bare feet, especially in the intertidal zone, and not even good for shell collectors because most of the shells are broken.

Regular beachcombers may notice that, on one day, there is an abundance of shells on the beach, while on the very next day many are gone, especially the larger conch shells. How did they disappear, and where did they go? This phenomenon is directly related to the type of wave striking the beach. Changes in wave height and shape can change the character of the shell exposure on the beach dramatically from day to day, week to week. A sudden increase in wave energy will lift the largest shells from their places on the beach and carry them seaward, where they will eventually settle on the shoreface, to be carried back to the beach in fair weather. Each beach is different in the way shells behave, and the scenario just described may vary a bit on your beach.

If you excavate a small ditch in a beach, you will discover that the beach is typically a layer cake of sand strata of different sizes. Interspersed among shell layers may be layers of finer sands and even a few very thin black layers of heavy minerals. This layering of the beach commonly is produced both by storms and by fair weather. At the peak of a storm, the uppermost few inches or feet of the beach are churned up with each passing wave. As the size and energy of the waves decrease, the coarsest material—that is, the shells—will settle out first, to be followed by finer sand. The result is a shelly layer in the beach. Swash from small waves may separate light and heavy sand grains, concentrating and leaving behind the thin dark layers of heavy minerals.

Some beach shell layers, however, may reflect quiet wave conditions. Shells may be concentrated in patches on the surface of the beach as wave swash removes finer beach sand under nonstorm conditions. The "pavement" of shells left behind is a called a *shell lag* (Fig. 6.3). These shell patches may subsequently be covered by fine beach sand under different wave conditions or tide levels, producing the layers observed in your beach excavation. Wind also may be involved in forming layers on the beach, especially the upper beach. Sorting out large and small grains from one another can produce both shell pavements and heavy mineral sand

Figure 6.2. These shells in Indian Beach were crushed by an off-road vehicle.

layers. Clearly, the layer cake that is the beach is a complex system formed by many processes.

You also may observe, in the wall of your excavated ditch, that some of the layers are crosscut or disrupted by different-colored or different-textured sand. Such disruptions show sediment reworking by burrowing animals, such as ghost crabs, as they move the sand to construct dwelling holes or to search for food.

Brown and Black Shells

All natural North Carolina open ocean beaches are light-brown to yellow-brown when viewed from afar. The brown color is due in significant part to brown shells, but few shells are naturally colored brown. If we look more closely at the shells in a beach, it is apparent that many are blackened.

Figure 6.3. The intertidal zone of Masonboro Island. Careful examination of this 2001 photo of a shell lag reveals that most of the clamshells are oriented concave down, with the cavity formerly occupied by the animal facing the beach surface. This orientation is the stable configuration of a clamshell on a beach with significant wave activity, whereas the stable configuration of a shell falling through the water column is concave up.

These colors, black and brown, are *secondary coloration*, meaning that the shell was stained a different color after its organism died (Plate 7).

How does a shell change from its original color to its secondary color? The brown shells seen on the Atlantic Coast receive their color when they are exposed to oxygen in the atmosphere. This leads to the oxidation of iron in the shells, leaving them a shade of brown. The iron oxide mineral formed in the interstices of the shell is *limonite*. Entire shells may be stained brown or sometimes just portions of them. The bottom line is that the beautiful brown coloration of all natural North Carolina ocean beaches is due to limonite deposition in seashells.

In stark contrast to the brown shells you observe, there are almost always some scattered black shells (Fig. 6.4). These have also undergone

Figure 6.4. A selection of shells from North Carolina beaches illustrating shell staining. The shells on the left are stained black as a result of burial in mud earlier in their history. On the right, the shells have their natural coloration.

secondary coloration, but of a different sort. Black shells were not stained on the beach but instead came from the backside of a barrier island, where they were deposited in the oxygen-poor muds of a lagoon or sound. Under these conditions of low oxygen, the iron in the shells turns into iron sulfide, which gives them their black color. At some point after the staining occurred, the barrier island migrated over the old lagoon deposits, and eventually the shells arrived on the beach.

To prove how shells become blackened, you can take fresh shells from the beach and bury them in mud, preferably salt-marsh mud. Within three to six weeks, most of them will have turned black. Some types of shells, such as the jingle shell, will blacken very quickly, whereas the oyster shell may take several weeks to change colors. Some, such as the scallop shell, may not blacken for months, if at all. Oysters are a particularly common black shell on our beaches. The beach at Ocracoke has a particularly large concentration of black shells.

In a general sense, the presence of black shells on a barrier island beach is proof that the island once migrated from a more seaward location. Brown shells are an infrequent component of continental shelf sands, but when they are found they are sure proof that the sediment at that location was once part of a beach, during a time of lower sea levels. Black shells, by contrast, are a very common component of the continental shelf sediment cover off North Carolina. These black shells indicate the former presence of a lagoon, and since a lagoon requires a barrier to hold off the open ocean, the shells provide evidence that barrier islands once existed out there on the shelf.

One must view shell-color evidence with caution, however. Bogue Banks, for example, now has a lot of black shells because of the beachfill projects of 2002 and 2003 that exhumed former estuary shells from their burial site on the continental shelf.

Although the process leading to brown staining occurs exclusively on beaches in North Carolina, the same is not true everywhere. For instance, on more southerly Caribbean shores like the north coast of Puerto Rico, brown staining occurs in the crystal-clear water on the sea floor between the shoreline and the two-hundred-foot depths. The color of these shells changes while they are still under water—a good example of why one must not transport generalizations about beaches very far from home!

On nourished beaches, the staining of shells does not reflect either local conditions or beach history. For example, at Wrightsville Beach, Carolina Beach, or Atlantic Beach, black shells may be unusually abundant while brown shells are absent. Brown shells are a rarity on nourished beaches. If the nourishment sand comes from a lagoon or old piles of dredged material, it will contain many black shells. On the other hand, if it comes from a nearby inlet (as is often the case on Wrightsville Beach), it may contain brown shells, because inlet sand is former beach sand, brought there by longshore currents in the surf zone. Because beach nourishment projects are becoming increasingly popular in communities confronted with retreating shorelines, fewer and fewer beaches in the future will have their original sand and shell components.

Brown staining does not occur rapidly, as black staining does. It is likely that a number of decades are required for shells on the beach to turn brown. Given current trends toward beach nourishment, the beautiful brown beaches of the Carolinas are an endangered species.

Shell Orientation

On the beach, clamshells are almost always positioned with the concave surface downward. That is, the cavity in which the animal once lived faces down toward the sand, and the outside of the shell faces up. But if such a shell is dropped into the water column of the surf zone, it will usually sink and land on the bottom in a concave upward orientation. That is, the shell will tend to land on what was formerly the exterior surface and the living cavity will face upward.

This means that the orientation of the shell as it falls through the water column is the reverse of the shell's orientation as it will normally end up on the beach (see Fig. 6.3). The reason for this difference is that the stable position for a shell on the beach, as the swash moves back and forth over it, is concave downward. You can easily test this idea by throwing shells into the swash zone and watching their behavior. Shells with the living cavity facing up will quickly be flipped over to their more stable position. On most North Carolina beaches, 90 percent or so of the whole clamshells will be oriented in this fashion.

Proving this to be the case is a neat beach exercise for students and for the curious beach stroller. First put on a face mask (with snorkel) and watch how a clamshell falls through the water column and settles on the bottom (you can also do this in an aquarium). Next, place some shells in the swash zone and watch them flip over to the stable concave downward orientation.

The very strong trend of preferred shell orientation on a beach is useful to geologists studying ancient beach and continental shelf sediments. Out on the continental shelf, starting a few miles from the beach, the orientation of clamshells is much more mixed. Shells may be oriented both concave up and concave down. Thus one criterion for distinguishing an ancient beach deposit from a deeper water sediment is the extent of preferred shell orientation.

There is another kind of shell orientation, and that is the direction of the long axis of long shells such as oysters. If you examine these shells on the surface of the beach, almost always there will be a preferred long-axis orientation with respect to waves or currents. To find out why, you need to observe how such shells are moved in the swash zone. Collect a few oyster shells and some spindle-shaped olive shells. Throw them into the swash zone. Does each type of shell take on similar orientations? The shape of the shell and its center of mass will determine how the swash wave moves and orients the shell. Different shapes are likely to have different orientations depending on how their shape is streamlined to the waves.

Sharks' Teeth

North Carolina is not well known for having large populations of sharks off its shores. But if you look long and hard enough, you can find fossil sharks' teeth on most of our beaches. Topsail Island is the best-known shore for sharks' teeth. A scoop of the pebble-sized gravel that makes up much of the beach on this barrier island will often contain a shiny black shark's tooth, usually smaller than $\frac{1}{4}''$ in length. Fossil sharks' teeth here have a shiny black surface with some streaks of a dark reddish-brown or dark gray color. A phosphate mineral has replaced the original material in the teeth, causing the color to change from creamy white to black. Searching for sharks' teeth usually requires time and patience. You're not likely to make any discoveries in your first scoop of shell hash, so sit down and enjoy prospecting.

The sharks' teeth found on Topsail are probably from the Miocene period, a geologic time that ranged from roughly twenty-five million to five million years ago. They come from slowly deteriorating rock outcrops on the continental shelf. Once a tooth is released to the sea floor, it is swept ashore by the waves, just like any seashell. Several species of sharks are represented, and occasionally shiny black phosphatic bone fragments can be found as well.

Macrofauna: Clams, Crabs, Turtles, Birds, and Other Large Creatures

Macrofauna is the term used for beach creatures that are visible to the naked eye, although some are pretty small. These animals include everything from clams and crabs to sea turtles, birds, and fish. A wide variety of animals live either in, on, or near the beach. Many others use North Carolina's beaches for nesting or feeding, or as a rest area while they are on their way to someplace else.

Living within the beach are several types of clams and crustaceans. Coquina clams (*Donax variabilis*) are among the most common. These tiny, wedge-shaped bivalves (two shells) live in the intertidal zone of the beach. About the size of a large fingernail, they come in many colors and live in dense groups of up to several hundred clams in one square foot of the beach. The outsides of the shells may be a completely different color from the inside, and some may have ringed, rayed, or solid color patterns. These clams, which have a patchy distribution, are efficient burrowers and disappear into the sand whenever the waves recede, but you can catch them fairly easily. After the death of the tenant, the two shells often open up but remain attached, giving the appearance of miniature butterfly wings.

Razor clams (*Tagelus* sp.) are also frequent residents in the intertidal beach sand. These creatures are long, narrow bivalves that, like coquina clams, can quickly burrow into the sand. *Tagelus* razor clams are usually less than three inches long. They look like old-fashioned straightedge razors, and they actually do have razor-sharp edges. These clams leave small, oval holes in the sand (but no piles of sand or droppings beside the hole opening). Although razor clams are edible, they are difficult to catch since they burrow so quickly. The Atlantic jackknife clam, or Atlantic razor clam, at up to six inches long, is the largest razor clam found on North

Carolina beaches. When its inhabitant is alive, the shell will be covered in a greenish-brown layer, which turns white after the clam dies. Fine, tan-colored growth rings may be visible on the shell, too.

In addition to the clams, there are many worms and crustaceans that live in our beaches. Most of the worms are not readily visible unless you dig around a lot in the wet sand. Mole crabs (*Emerita* sp.), good burrowers that move about in the swash zone much like the coquina clams, are easy to spot. They are small (one-half to one inch), grayish-tan animals without pincers that rapidly bury themselves in wet sand when the waves recede. Mole crabs dig small burrows in the swash zone, where they stick antennae-like stalks up into the backwash to filter out food; these creatures are sometimes used as bait by surf fishermen. Coquina clams, mole crabs, and worms are a source of food for many birds and fish that frequent the beach.

Ghost shrimp (*Callianasa* sp.) live in the beach, too, leaving larger holes with small mounds of sand surrounding the opening (Figs. 6.5 and 6.6). This extra pile of sand consists of both waste products and excavated materials. Ghost shrimp burrows never begin at a higher elevation than the mid-tide position on the beach. Geologists have used this fact to determine former sea levels by measuring the maximum elevation of ghost shrimp burrows. These creatures can burrow up to six feet into the sand. North Carolina is near the northern limit of these animals' habitat, and they are much more common in South Carolina and Georgia beaches.

Up on the drier part of the beach, out of the intertidal zone, you might come across ghost crabs (*Ocypode quadrata*). Ghost crabs are camouflaged so as to blend in with the sand when they stand still, but it is easy to spot them scurrying across the sand between the water and their burrows. Able to run in just about any direction, these little crustaceans (up to several inches big) have white pincers and underbellies and periscope-type eyes mounted on stalks. They steal birds' eggs and eat coquina clams, mole crabs, and other animals (dead or alive) found on the beach, but they must occasionally visit the water to rewet their gills. Ghost crabs tend to be more active at night but are just as ghostly when seen in the daylight. At one to three inches wide, the burrow holes of ghost crabs are larger than those of other beach critters (Fig. 6.7). These burrows may extend up to

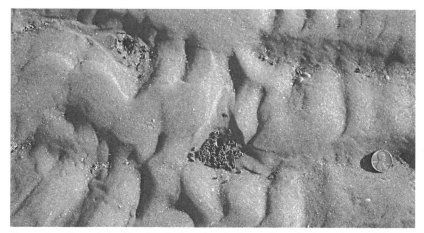

Figure 6.5. Ghost shrimp fecal pellets. A close look reveals perfectly uniform cylinders of mud accumulated in depressions of the ladder-back ripples. A small ghost shrimp burrow is visible in the upper left of the photo. Penny for scale.

Figure 6.6. A ghost shrimp burrow that has been excavated by wind or water. Note the adhesion ripple surface formed as dry sand blows over wet sand. Penny for scale.

four feet into the sand and provide a shelter during the winter when the crabs are dormant. Ghost crabs are another good living indicator of a disturbed beach. They tend to be less abundant or absent entirely on bulldozed beaches or those heavily visited by people. Brunswick County

Figure 6.7. A typical ghost crab burrow in the wrack line on the upper beach of Ocean Isle. When excavated, these burrows prove to have multiple chambers and more than one opening, and they extend as deep as four feet. The crab has recently carried out housekeeping and has deposited sand, carried into the hole by wind and swash, on the beach around its hole. Quarter for scale.

beaches that have not been bulldozed or nourished are usually a good place to find these crabs, as are the Cape Hatteras and Cape Lookout National Seashores.

While all the critters mentioned up to this point actually live on or in the beach (ghost crabs also burrow into the frontal dunes), there are many others that visit the beach just to nest or feed. The wrack line provides a convenient source of food for many animals, as do some of the macrofauna that live in the wet sand.

Both sea turtles and horseshoe crabs venture out of the water to nest on North Carolina beaches. They dig holes in the dry sand in which to lay and bury their eggs. Five different types of sea turtles have been known to visit North Carolina waters, all of them endangered or threatened species. The loggerhead (*Caretta caretta*) is the most common sea turtle to lay nests in

Figure 6.8. Tracks left behind by a female loggerhead sea turtle on Lea Island in July 2002 after she finished laying a nest of eggs. A loggerhead sea turtle nest in North Carolina typically contains 100 to 125 eggs.

North Carolina (about a thousand a year). Sea turtle nests are more abundant along the state's southern coast, with about a hundred on Oak Island during any given summer but less than a dozen north of Oregon Inlet.

Sea turtles are amazing creatures. They can swim at speeds of over one mile per hour for long periods of time and up to twenty miles per hour for short distances. A mother loggerhead turtle that climbs out of the water to nest at night may weigh between two hundred and five hundred pounds and be over three feet long. She may lay more than one hundred eggs in any given nest and nest a few times in any nesting season. Loggerhead turtle nests are buried about two feet below the surface of the beach, near the toe of a dune. Nests are laid between May and September, with hatching continuing into November. The mother turtle never takes care of the eggs once they are buried but leaves the nest for Mother Nature to watch over. When they dig up out of their nests in the late summer and fall, new hatchlings head for the sea but may get confused by house and street lights.

If you are walking on a beach shortly after dawn, and the tide has not

Figure 6.9. Carapace (shell) of a horseshoe crab, a common sight on North Carolina beaches. Horseshoe crabs molt, shed their carapaces, and grow new ones. Most of those found on the beaches are actually molts and not dead crabs.

come in yet, you may see turtle tracks (Fig. 6.8). These are the flipper-prints left behind as the female turtle returned to the sea, and they look a bit like ATV tire tracks except they head straight into the water! Don't disturb the nest she may have left behind, but report it to the local sea turtle watch program. Every island seems to have a "turtle lady" or a volunteer sea turtle group. There is also a sea turtle hospital on Topsail Island where injured turtles are rehabilitated and later returned to the sea.

Horseshoe crabs (*Limulus* sp.) might be familiar to you if you have found their large, brown carapaces washed up on the beach. These "bodies" are usually molts shed as the animals grow (Fig. 6.9). These animals aren't really crabs as their name implies, but they belong to the same general group of animals. They also are related to the long-extinct trilobites, and their geologic record goes back a few hundred million years. So if you think they have an "ancient" look about them, they do! Horseshoe crabs move around on five sets of legs and use their tails to flip themselves over

Table 6.2. Common Bird Species on North Carolina Beaches

American oystercatcher	Laughing gull
Black skimmer	Least tern
Brown pelican	Northern gannet
Caspian tern	Piping plover
Common tern	Red knot
Double-crested cormorant	Ring-billed gull
Dowitcher (short-billed	Royal tern
and long-billed)	Ruddy turnstone
Dunlin	Sanderlings
Forster's tern	Sandpipers
Great black-backed gull	Semipalmated plover
Gull-billed tern	Willet
Herring gull	Wilson's plover
Killdeer	Yellowlegs (greater and lesser)

Note: Hundreds of species of birds can be found on and near North Carolina beaches; this table lists some of the most common species. Colonial waterbirds nest in groups, or colonies, while shorebirds do not nest in groups. Terns, brown pelicans, and black skimmers are colonial waterbirds, and plovers, American oystercatchers, and willets are shorebirds. Both colonial waterbirds and shorebirds nest on bare sand, especially in overwash areas and near inlets. North Carolina beaches provide habitats for nesting as well as for foraging and resting while birds are migrating north and south or overwintering.

if they end up knocked on their backs by a wave. They live in waters ranging anywhere from the shoreline to a depth of seventy-five feet, plowing through the bottom sediments looking for food. Like sea turtles, horseshoe crabs lay and bury a huge number of eggs in shallow holes on the beach, up to ten times each spring and summer. The difference is that they lay their eggs on estuarine instead of ocean beaches. Their eggs are an important source of food for migrating shorebirds.

Finally, a multitude of birds visit North Carolina's beaches to eat or nest (Table 6.2). There are hundreds of species of shorebirds and waterbirds to be found on the North Carolina shore. The two most common birds that you will spot running about in the swash zone, feeding on the clams

Figure 6.10. Sanderlings are one of the most common birds seen running around in the waves, looking for food. This sanderling was foraging in the swash at Pea Island National Wildlife Refuge. (Sidney Maddock Photography)

and other creatures that live in the sand, are sanderlings and willets. Sanderlings (*Calidris alba*) are small, gray- to brown-colored birds with white bellies (Fig. 6.10). Sometimes they are more rust-colored than gray during the summer. They have black beaks and legs. These enthusiastic birds run up and down the beach between the waves, often in groups or flocks. Although you are almost assured of seeing them on our beaches during any season of the year, they actually breed far away in the polar regions. North Carolina is an important place for sanderlings during the winter, though, with the state being home to some of the highest concentrations of birds on the East Coast.

Willets (*Catoptrophorus semipalmatus*) live alongside the sanderlings, feeding in the swash zone between waves (Fig. 6.11). But they are larger, almost a foot tall with longer legs and beaks. These shorebirds are gray in the winter and brown in summer, with a distinctive black-bordered white stripe on their wings that is visible when they fly. If you startle one into flight, it may utter some piercing cries at you as it flies away. Unlike the sanderlings, willets nest on North Carolina beaches as well as feed here. They build their nests either in the secondary dunes or near the marshes.

Figure 6.11. Willets feed in the swash zone. This one was spotted after it found a mole crab to eat in Pea Island National Wildlife Refuge. (Sidney Maddock Photography)

Beware, though, that willets are very protective of their nests and will make a great ruckus if you approach one!

In addition to sanderlings and willets, dozens of other types of shorebirds use North Carolina beaches for nesting, foraging, shelter, and just loafing. Intertidal shoals near inlets are a favorite habitat for many resting and feeding birds. Wilson's plover (*Charadrius wilsonia*), American oystercatcher (*Haematopus palliatus*), and occasionally the piping plover (*Charadrius melodus*), a threatened and endangered species, nest on bare sand in overwash areas or near inlets. Colonial waterbirds also nest on bare ground and use dredge disposal islands and sometimes the flat roofs of large buildings for nesting in addition to inlet and overwash areas. Colonial waterbirds nest in large groups, with up to hundreds of nests spaced closely together. Black skimmers (*Rynchops niger*), common terns (*Sterna hirundo*), and least terns (*Sterna antillarum*) frequently nest together in these large colonies. Many of their nest sites are roped off and signposted

Figure 6.12. Many birds congregate in flocks on intertidal shoals, especially during the spring and fall migratory seasons. These black skimmers are grouped on intertidal shoals near Mason Inlet before the inlet's relocation in 2002. (Walker Golder Photography)

during the late spring and early summer to minimize human and pet disturbance of the nesting birds.

During the spring and fall, the diversity of birds on North Carolina beaches often increases as thousands of birds fly through the state on their way north (in the spring) or south (in the fall). These migratory birds may stop over on our beaches and inlets to rest and stock up on food, or they may pass through quickly without any long stops (Fig. 6.12). North Carolina is the final destination for some of these birds, who may spend their summers in Canada and return to our coastal areas for overwintering. North Carolina is a unique place for birdwatching because our beaches overlap the breeding and overwintering ranges for several species of birds, and you can find dozens of types of birds here year-round.

Clearly, the beach is full of living things, as you can prove if you stop and take a look! In addition to the live creatures you can observe, the multitude of shells left on a beach are clues to the many other creatures living beyond the beach beneath the waves, as well as those that called these sands home thousands of years ago.

Meiofauna: Microscopic Critters in the Sand

Big critters are not the only ones who like living on the shore. If you are standing on the beach, beneath one of your footprints in the sand could be thousands of living things that you can't even see. One square yard of low-tide beach alone may be home to something on the order of one million organisms. These organisms, which live in the cavities between grains of sand, are collectively known as *meiofauna*. An incredible number of meiofaunal species exist on the beach, and numbers of individuals representing a single species within the sand are often awesome. Meiofauna are defined by their size—small, smaller, and smallest. They range in length anywhere from 0.045 to 0.5 millimeters, too small to see with the naked eye. But they are down there, everywhere, as the birds prancing in the surf zone know well.

Meiofauna is a nonspecific term referring to a large group of often unrelated animals. The main requirement for an organism to be included in the meiofauna category is the ability to move through the sand without displacing the individual sand grains. Typically, meiofauna have an elongate shape that allows them to maneuver successfully between the grains. Some meiofauna have what appear to be legs. But to move, these creatures use gliding or writhing motions.

These organisms have evolved over time to adapt to the tight quarters of their habitat. Over generations, the size of the cells in meiofauna creatures has decreased to better suit them for occupying their tiny homes. So the grain size of the beach sand is the most important factor in determining where these animals end up living.

Most meiofauna are found in the upper inch of the sand, right there by your bare feet. If you were to scoop up a handful of sand, you might have more than twenty different species in the mound that sits in your hand. Nematodes compose up to 85 percent of the species in the meiofauna, and

Table 6.3. Federally Endangered and Threatened Species That Utilize North Carolina Coastal Habitats

BIRDS

Piping plover (*Charadrius melodus*)
Roseate tern (*Sterna dougallii*)

REPTILES

Loggerhead sea turtle (*Caretta caretta*)
Green sea turtle (*Chelonia mydas*)
Kemp's Ridley sea turtle (*Lepidochelys kempii*)
Leatherback sea turtle (*Dermochelys coriacea*)
Hawksbill sea turtle (*Retmochelys imbricata imbricata*)

PLANTS

Seabeach amaranth (*Amaranthus pumilus*)

they play an important role in the beach ecology because they feed mostly on bacteria, algae, detritus (broken-up organic material), and dissolved organic matter. In other words, they clean up the beach by filtering the water. Occasionally they will prey on other microscopic animals. But for the most part, nematodes are not predators.

After nematodes, *Harpacticoida* sp. is often the most abundant type of meiofauna in the sand. Scientists have found *Harpacticoida* sp. in the stomach contents of some species of bottom-feeding fish, which appear to filter the animals out of the beach or continental shelf sands.

The meiofauna have the potential to be used as an indicator of pollution on beaches. But they have not been studied much in the United States. These organisms are extremely sensitive to environmental change and have relatively short lifespans. Their presence or absence in a beach may also be a partial indicator of the environmental impact of beach bulldozing and beach nourishment. Given their microscopic size, we have to leave the reading of this part of the beach record to the experts with microscopes.

Figure 6.13. Extensive off-road vehicle tracks on an Outer Banks beach. These tracks may kill many beach organisms, make it difficult for beach strollers to walk, and are unsightly in terms of beach aesthetics.

Natural Beaches and Their Biota: An Uncertain Future

Every time a species disappears from one of its former habitats, and particularly when a species goes extinct, nature's alarm is sounding. Table 6.3 lists several endangered and threatened animals that rely on North Carolina beaches for their survival. Beaches are vital to a large ecosystem, to a huge number of organisms including the seabirds we love to watch and the fish we love to catch. The seashells we love to find are also endangered because of vehicular traffic (Fig. 6.13). The dilemma is how to love our beaches, but not love them to death.

Conservation of Beaches

The previous chapters have demonstrated that there is a lot more to North Carolina's beaches than meets the eye. The beaches evolve in a fascinating hodge-podge of biological and physical processes, modern and ancient, that we barely understand. The fact that there is so much yet to learn makes beaches all the more alluring.

In this chapter we are probably preaching to the saved, because the chances are that if you've read this far in the book (and didn't cheat by trying to find out the ending before finishing), you are already a beach-lover. You don't need to be convinced that North Carolina's beaches are priceless. You probably also know that our beautiful beaches are in trouble. No one needs to prove to you that we have a problem. The frequency and number of articles and reports in the media about beach erosion, beach nourishment, and beachfront development/environment conflicts attest to the fact that something foul is afoot. In addition, if you have been going down to the beach for a number of years, a decade or more, you have probably noted that the buildings near the beach have increased in both size and number, and you have observed that the shoreline has gotten closer to the buildings (Plate 8). If you have walked far enough along your beach, you have probably seen a number of sandbag seawalls or some dunes made up of shelly sand—a dead giveaway that they are bulldozed piles of sand. You might even have seen some bulldozers in action or perhaps their tracks. If you came down to your beach in the spring, your trek to the water may have been blocked by a long line of pipes moving sand to a point from which it was spewed onto the beach. And if you've encountered this type of project, you may have been surprised and disappointed by the new color of your beach, or by the angular

Figure 7.1. Northern New Jersey before the introduction of a $200 million beachfill. The beach shown here is the endpoint of more than a hundred years of holding the shoreline in place. This is what we want to prevent in North Carolina.

shell debris or coarse material that detracted from your recreational use of the beach.

In fact, your impression may be that the beaches of North Carolina have turned into giant engineering projects. Is this what we want for our beaches—to be regarded and treated as no more than another community infrastructure on a par with roads, sewer lines, and telephone poles? There is a difference!

Beach retreat is not a new discovery. North Carolinians have been coping with the effects of sea-level rise since colonial times. But the practice of building communities right next to the beach is a new phenomenon. Early Outer Banks settlements as well as the first resorts at Nags Head were all located on the backsides of the islands, as far as possible from the beach. But development encroached toward the beach, and the sea did the same. By the mid-twentieth century it was clear that we were heading for an erosion problem.

The biggest single threat to beach survival is shoreline armoring (Fig 7.1). Construction of seawalls and groins always leads to the loss of beaches in the next generation or two. In 1985 North Carolina was a pioneer in farsighted coastal management, strictly regulating construction of new shoreline armoring (Fig. 7.2). Unfortunately, nature tested the regulations by backing shorelines right up to expensive homes owned by politically influential people, and the regulations were found wanting. The state compromised by allowing installation of temporary seawalls made of sandbags (see Plate 8), but as far as the beach is concerned, there is no difference between a sandbag wall and a concrete wall. In the meantime, the original temporary two-year time limit for the "temporary" walls has long since expired. Only storms have removed the walls, but all the while, more sandbag walls are being built. Limits have been defeated by variances and by officials who have allowed "temporary" to mean "permanent." Along with the beaches, the political will to conserve one of the state's most important resources has also eroded.

What's Up?

What's up? Well, the number of buildings is increasing along our North Carolina shorelines because we are in the middle of a giant rush to the sea. The scramble to the beach is fueled by a society with a lot of money, a love for the sea and a desire to live beside it, a greedy development industry, an irresponsible real estate industry, local governments anxious to create more tax revenue and employ more local citizens, and a contempt for the forces of nature. Sea level continues to rise, moving the shoreline ever closer to the buildings. All over the world, whether they are developed or not, shorelines are retreating in a landward direction.

Most likely sea level is rising in part because of the greenhouse effect. Increasing amounts of carbon dioxide and other compounds are accumulating in the atmosphere at an accelerating rate, and the atmosphere is being warmed. Glaciers all over the world are receding at alarming rates, melting and contributing "new" water to the oceans. The warming atmosphere is heating and expanding the oceans' surface water, which also leads to higher sea level. It is clear that the most recent jump in the rate of sea-level rise, which began perhaps a hundred years ago, is here to stay. Sea level will continue to rise, and most likely that rise will accelerate in coming years.

Figure 7.2. An old seawall or bulkhead on Caswell Beach that was destroyed by Hurricane Bonnie in 1998. A house once protected by the structure is now gone. Holding the shoreline in place by structures such as these leads eventually to the destruction of the beach.

So What?

The standard question all good research scientists ask when their results are in is, "So what?" Shorelines will continue to retreat toward and beyond the houses, and beachfront property owners will become more and more desperate as their buildings threaten to tumble into the sea. Well, "So what? That's their problem," you might say. "Why should it worry me?" You should be worried because, in order to solve their problem, they create problems for the rest of us who use the beach. Beachfront property owners are a very small number of citizens compared with the number who use the beach. Yet they control the fate of the public domain—our beach. And what they are doing to your beach is destructive both environmentally and, in the long term, economically.

From a short-term economic standpoint, owning a beachfront house makes sense. Individuals and companies own many such buildings for the sole purpose of making money—an old and respectable American tradition. In this sense, the North Carolina beachfront is a giant cash cow. No doubt about it, however, by most other measures of societal and personal responsibility, owning a beachfront house is imprudent, if not irrational. Stan Riggs, a geologist at East Carolina University, has suggested that owning beachfront property is akin to having a picnic on an interstate highway, an image meant to convey how irrational it is to put your property as well as yourself and others at risk.

Whether these property owners are irresponsible or irrational, the real problem is that a massive and costly effort will be carried out to hold the shoreline in place when their buildings are threatened with falling into the sea. These efforts to fix the shoreline are well under way in North Carolina. Almost every beach community is doing some bulldozing to form artificial dunes, a process that kills all the critters in the upper beach and is in itself a form of beach erosion. In most communities there are buildings located right out on the beach, interfering with your beach activities and dramatically decreasing the aesthetics of the beach. On at least ten beaches, the sand you play on no longer has the beautiful brown coloration of a native North Carolina beach because that sand has been brought in from somewhere else and pumped up onto the beach (a few more dead critters). And in ever increasing numbers, sandbag seawalls are appearing along the beaches, ultimately contributing to their degradation (Figs. 7.3 and 7.4). Your beach has become the playground of engineers.

Well, why not save these beachfront buildings? Is it reasonable just to let them fall into the sea? We are a society of great engineering skill. We build levees to protect property along rivers and dams to control river flow, and we construct buildings to resist earthquakes. Why not build seawalls or artificial dunes to protect property along beaches? Why walk away from an engineering solution?

First, let's examine that question from the standpoint of global warming. The erosion of our shorelines in North Carolina became an "erosion problem" when buildings were threatened. It is important to distinguish between erosion and an erosion problem. This erosion problem may be the first large-scale and global impact of the greenhouse effect. We are already seeing major losses of important wetlands in the Mississippi Delta, and it may not be long until such climate changes will affect agriculture in

Figure 7.3. Sandbags protecting houses in South Nags Head in 2000. No dry beach remains, and there is not even a wet beach over much of the tidal cycle. In terms of loss of the beach, sandbags are no different from concrete seawalls.

the U.S. Midwest. Should we roll with the punches of the greenhouse effect, or should we try to engineer our way out of them? In the Mississippi Delta, plans are afoot to hold the shorelines in place and keep everybody happy to the tune of billions of dollars per decade. In the Midwest, we hear talk of bringing irrigation water from the Great Lakes to newly parched fields so farmers can continue to grow the same corn crops that they always have. But why not change crops, and why not accept marsh loss? Why insist on the status quo? Is it even possible to sustain an engineered society that is out of context with its environment?

The status quo is what we in North Carolina attempt to maintain when we accept the principle that beachfront houses should be saved. But why should we pay a huge price to save the property of a small number of people who were so ignorant or arrogant that they built right next to an

Figure 7.4. Remnants of sandbags, pavement fragments, and construction debris from a house and driveway that fell in on Holden Beach in March 2002. Sandbags are readily destroyed by storms and thus are frequently replaced. There has been little attempt by local, state, or federal government to require cleanup of such material on the beach. As a consequence, sandbag remnants in particular are a widespread beach feature in North Carolina.

eroding shoreline? Aside from this philosophical problem, the next question is, why should we pay through our federal government to bail them out of the consequences of their imprudent actions? Why don't *they* pay to hold the shoreline in place?

Right now we are planning to continue nourishing our beaches. We have a plan rolling along to nourish essentially every beach in North Carolina that has buildings on it. "Rolling along" is putting it mildly. The North Carolina beach nourishment program is akin to a juggernaut hurtling down a steep hill. But some beaches—for example, those at Figure Eight Island and Kill Devil Hills—have little nearby sand to use on the beach. More important, however, is that as sea levels rise the erosion rates of nourished beaches will become ever greater, and the cost of keeping artificial beaches in place will be ever higher. The quality of sand used will diminish as well. Already we have two "bad" nourished beaches, one that

Figure 7.5. An erosion scarp on the new rock-hard beach at Pine Knoll Shores in February 2002. Although the surface of this beach eventually became sandy, the intertidal zone where people swim will likely be filled with fragmental shells for years to come. The beach was approved by both the State Division of Coastal Management and the U.S. Army Corps of Engineers. North Carolinians must make every effort to prevent such beach nourishment failures in the future.

Figure 7.6. The new beach at Oak Island contained abundant rock cobbles the size of grapefruits in May 2002. This beach was specifically funded by the federal government as a sea turtle habitat restoration project, the first of its kind in North Carolina. The cobbles in the beach obviously hinder both turtle nesting and people's swimming activities.

is too shelly (Pine Knoll Shores) and one that contains abundant grapefruit-sized rocks (Oak Island) (Figs. 7.5, 7.6, and 7.7). Most likely, within two to three generations the sea-level rise will force us to give up on nourishment and build massive seawalls. By that time, national priorities will have moved on to saving sea-level cities such as New Orleans, Miami, Manhattan, and Boston, and the Wrightsville Beaches and Nags Heads will have moved to society's back burner.

Adding to this problem is the fact that nourished beaches lead to greatly

Figure 7.7. Balls of clay were contained within the fill material pumped onto Ocean Isle in 2001.

increased property values, which in turn encourages builders to replace single-family houses with larger, multifamily units lining the shore. High-rises will quickly supplant beach cottages. It's already happening at Carolina Beach—all because of the beach nourishment. Once a beach is lined with highrises, all flexibility of response to the sea-level rise is forfeited. The future giant seawall becomes a certainty.

The loss of the natural beach is also an environmental disaster. This physical buffer offers storm protection while acting as the coastal conduit of sand that supplies a wide range of ecosystems. We have seen that the beach is the critical interface between land and sea as well as an ecosystem unto itself. Even beach nourishment, often sold as "working with nature," takes a heavy toll on plant and animal species. In the end, artificial beaches and dunes are just that—artificial, rather than the dynamic natural order that sustained the ecosystem.

What's the Alternative?

We can decide not to defend the status quo and begin making decisions based on the interests of all who use our beaches. If we decide that beaches are more important than buildings, we can let the shoreline retreat and let the buildings fall in when their time comes. Or we can move the buildings back. Or we can move them off-island, or even initiate planned gradual demolishment. If we do any of these things, we will save the beaches for our descendants. A study of beach nourishment alternatives in Dare County showed that purchasing beachfront property outright would be far cheaper than nourishing the beach over a time span of several decades. The technology to move buildings, even substantial ones, exists. Entire communities have been moved out of floodplains.

Actually, if we really put our hearts and our pocketbooks into it, we could eventually save the beachfront houses in the Dutch fashion, with massive seawalls and dikes. But the environmental and economic price would be huge, and we would leave no beaches behind for our great-grandchildren.

There is little in-between breathing space. Once we start nourishing a beach, or once we build a seawall, there is no turning back. Historically, we rarely reverse our course when it comes to shoreline engineering. We can, for example, fine-tune the retreat from the shoreline with some beach nourishment. And when we nourish the beach, we could require that beach cottages must remain just that—no highrise jungles allowed. That would allow the next generation to reevaluate the strategy for saving beaches.

Right now, it is up to the citizens of North Carolina to decide what's more important: buildings or beaches? The greatest riddle of all may be, "What did we destroy because we loved it so much?"

Beach Terminology

accretion: The addition of sand to a beach, allowing it to widen and build out seaward.

adhesion structure: Bedform produced by dry sand sticking to and accumulating on a wet surface to form irregular, wartlike features or small, irregular ripples.

antidune: Long, low, asymmetric ridge of sand (megaripple), several inches high, with its steep face oriented opposite the direction of flow. Antidunes are formed by the seaward return of the swash over fine-grained sand, usually on a steep portion of the beach.

armored mud ball: An eroded piece of coherent mud will become rounded when rolled over the beach by waves and swash. This mud ball becomes "armored" when sand and shell debris stick to its outer surface, reducing the chance of the mud ball's being destroyed by abrasion.

backshore: The portion of the beach landward of the normal high-tide line.

beach scraping: A bulldozing procedure in which a layer of sand (legally less than one foot thick) is pushed from the intertidal zone and forebeach to the back part of the beach to form an artificial "dune."

bedform: A small-scale feature formed on the surface of the beach. Bedforms may be preserved by burial or wiped out with the next tide. Examples include ripple marks and trails of organisms.

berm: A depositional terracelike feature on the upper beach.

berm crest: The seaward limit of the berm beyond which is the steep berm face.

black sand: Heavy-mineral concentrations or placers that form by the winnowing away (by wind or water) of the lighter sand grains. The black color typically comes from magnetite and ilmenite. Commonly mistaken for oil pollution.

blister: A dome-shaped feature formed by air trapped between sand layers within the beach.

blowout: A flat or bowl-shaped area in a dune field where dune sand has been blown away (eroded). The wind often erodes down to the level of the water table, where wet sand prevents more erosion.

bubbly sand: Sand with an open, porous texture due to the entrapment of air bubbles within the beach.

crescent mark: The scour mark around an object on the beach, such as a shell or pebble, resulting from wind or water flow around the object.

cross-bedding: The thin, inclined laminations that form in a dune. Successive laminations show different orientations.

current ripples: Ripple marks that are short-crested and formed by water current flow such as in a trough (runnel) on the beach. Such ripple marks are described by their shape (linguoid, cuspate, lunate, catenary).

cusps: Crescent-shaped troughs separated by mounds or low ridges that extend seaward and that occur at regular intervals along the beach.

drag mark: A line or pattern on the surface of the beach, produced when the wind or the swash drags an object over the surface. Drag marks are produced by shell fragments, clumps of seaweed, and other wrack.

dredging: The removal of sand by dredges to improve a natural channel for boat traffic or to provide a sand supply for beach nourishment.

drift line: A mass of natural and artificial debris (e.g., seaweed, *Spartina* straw, fishing nets, lumber, driftwood, plastic bottles) indicating the previous landward extent of the high-tide line and/or wave swash.

dune: A land feature formed from an accumulation of windblown sand, either bare or covered with vegetation.

dynamic equilibrium: Natural balance between the processes and materials to produce a land form. In the case of a beach, its profile is a function of sea-level change, wave energy, and sediment supply.

ebb current: The tidal current formed when the tide is "going out."

ebb tidal delta: The body of sand that protrudes seaward of an inlet formed by ebb tidal currents.

erosion: The net loss of sand from a beach that leads to the retreat of the shoreline.

fetch: The distance of open water over which the wind can blow to form waves.

flaser ripples: Ripples characterized by mud accumulation in their troughs, resulting in interbedded sand/mud.

flat-topped ripples: Ripples on which the tops or crests are flattened as a result of the reversal of the current or wave direction producing the structure (e.g., changing tide).

flood current: The tidal current formed as the tide is rising.

flood tidal delta: The body of sand, landward of an inlet, formed by flood-tidal currents.

foam: The bubbly froth on the surface of the sea formed by waves mixing fine organic and mud debris with air.

foam stripes: Parallel tracks of microfurrows and rims formed where a patch of foam moved across the beach.

foam tracks: Bubble traces where an individual bubble or patch of bubbles was in contact with the beach. Patterns vary from stripes to patches.

foredune: The dune closest to the beach.

foreshore: The seaward dipping zone on a beach between high- and low-tide levels.

groin: An engineering structure installed perpendicular to the beach in an effort to trap sand traveling with the longshore current. Shorter than jetties, groins are almost always placed in groups (or fields). Groins cause sand accretion on the updrift side, but erosion on the downdrift side.

groundwater: The freshwater stored underground. On a beach, the groundwater table meets the sea and helps influence the coastal processes occurring there.

heavy minerals: The mineral fraction of beaches consisting of grains that are heavier than quartz and feldspar (the light minerals).

inner bar: The landward of two or more sandbars found off a beach.

interference ripples: Pattern of two or more sets of ripple marks that are running into each other; produced by changing wind, wave, and current conditions.

intertidal zone: The wet portion of the beach exposed at low tide. The zone between the low and the high tides.

jetty: Long navigation structures perpendicular to the shore, usually placed in pairs on the sides of inlets to stabilize a navigational channel and to prevent sediment transported by longshore currents from clogging the channel (e.g., Masonboro Inlet).

ladder-back ripples: Compound ripple marks produced when one set of ripple marks forms atop a previous set at nearly a right angle, producing a stepladder pattern. Produced by changing wave directions during the falling tide and usually found on tidal flats.

littoral drift: Also known as longshore sediment transport, littoral drift is the movement of sand along a beach due to waves striking the beach at an angle. Most beaches in North Carolina have littoral drift from north to south, but storms and seasons can reverse the direction of drift. The "net littoral drift" is the dominant direction of sediment movement (or the volume of sand moved in one direction minus the volume moved in the other direction) over a year's time.

longshore current: The current flowing parallel to a beach that is created by waves striking the coast at an angle.

macrofauna: Beach animals visible to the naked eye. The animals living on or in the beach including coquina clams, razor clams, ghost shrimp, ghost crabs, and various types of worms.

medaño: A large, solitary dune such as Jockey's Ridge or Run Hill Dune that is created by winds blowing from several different directions.

meiofauna: Microscopic-sized animals that live between sand grains in the beach.

nail hole: An informal term for a hole in the beach that has the diameter of a nail. Such holes are produced by air escaping from the sand.

neap tide: The minimum tidal range at a beach (least difference between high and low tides), occurring during the first or third quarters of the moon.

nourished beach: An artificial beach that has been widened or maintained by the import of new sediment; more accurately termed beachfill.

offshore bar: A ridge of sand under the water off the beach, usually identifiable by breaking waves.

offshore breakwater: An engineered structure placed offshore and parallel to the beach. Breakwaters mimic sandbars to cause waves to break, lessening erosion on the beach behind the breakwater but interrupting the longshore drift.

outer bar: The outermost of two or more sandbars on a beach. The biggest waves break on this seaward-most bar.

overwash: Beach sand that has been transported inland beyond the beach by storm waves.

overwash fan: An accumulation of sand and shells (often fan shaped) that is deposited by overwash, usually in a splay or fan shape.

parting lineation: The pattern or fabric of the surface of the berm face produced by the swash orientation of the grains. Usually found in association with swash marks and other swash features.

pedestal: Column structure formed by wind erosion where a resistant object, such as a shell, holds the underlying sand in place.

pit: Any depression on the beach or dune that lacks a rim such as is found in a sand volcano. Pits have a variety of origins.

plant arc: An arc-shaped ring or other traced pattern in the sand produced by the wind movement of the end of a plant frond, leaf, or rootlet.

plunging breaker: A wave that breaks on a moderate beach slope (usually 3–11°). The breaker curls over, forming a barrel or tube of air as it collapses. The most forceful type of breaker in terms of generating sand movement on the seafloor.

positive interference: When two (or more) waves from different sources meet in phase (crest to crest or trough to trough). The resulting wave is the combined height of the two original waves.

quicksand: Sand that liquefies when disturbed due to a change in the packing of the grains. Bubbly sand will behave in this manner when vibrated as the trapped bubbles collapse.

raindrop impression: Pit formed by the impact of a raindrop on sand.

rhomboid ripples: Diamond-shaped ripple marks created by the wave swash during retreating tides.

ridge and runnel: The "ridge" of a ridge and runnel system is a sandbar. The "runnel" is the troughlike area between the ridge and the beach.

rill marks: Small erosional channels in the sand carved out by either fresh- or saltwater draining out of the beach sand at low tide. At the end of each rill the sand is deposited in small splays or microdelta-like features.

ring structure: Circular pattern formed on beach surface when a blister is truncated and the layers of different-colored sand are exposed.

rip current: A fast-moving flow of water from the beach seaward through the surf zone.

ripple marks: Small-scale ridges and depressions in the sand, typically in a repetitive pattern. Different patterns are created by different air, water, and wave conditions.

rogue wave: A rare wave formed by the convergence and positive interference of several different waves. As wave trains meet each other, waves that are in phase (crest to crest and trough to trough) combine into much larger waves (positive interference).

salcrete: Layer of cohesive sand on the surface of the beach that sticks together due to cementation by salt crystals.

sand: Grains of material (minerals such as quartz or magnetite, or bits of shells) that range in size from $1/16$ to 2 millimeters in diameter.

sandbar: *See* offshore bar.

scarp: A small sand cliff on the beach indicating rapid erosion.

sea: The choppy, irregular (confused) water surface formed when waves are locally generated.

sea level: The average elevation of the water surface of the sea.

seawall: An engineered wall on the upper beach, installed parallel to the beach in an effort to prevent retreat of the shoreline and erosion of property.

sedimentary structures: General category including surface bedforms and internal beach and dune structures like cross-bedding, produced by sedimentary agents such as waves and currents.

shell hash: Descriptive term for a concentration of broken shell material on a beach.

singing/squeaking sand: Any sand that produces sound when walked on; most often dry sand at the back of the beach.

softsand: Sand that yields under pressure due to the collapse of trapped air bubbles.

spilling breaker: A wave that breaks on a relatively flat beach slope (typically 3° or less). The wave crest literally spills over the top of the wave but does not curl like a plunging breaker.

spring tide: The highest tidal range at a beach, occurring during a full or new moon.

storm surge: The rise in water level due to the low atmospheric pressure at the center of a storm, water mounding due to circulation around the low-pressure center, and the effect of water being pushed onshore into shallower depths.

surf zone: The band of water adjacent to the beach over which waves are breaking.

surging breaker: A wave that comes ashore on a steep bottom slope (generally greater than 11°) but does not break like spilling or plunging breakers.

swash: The final remains of a wave as it rolls up on the beach.

swash mark: Line formed at the edge of swash advance when a wave breaks. As water soaks into the beach, the material being carried by the swash or floating on its edge is deposited to form the line.

swash zone: The area of the beach over which wave swash is running up and down the beach.

swell: Evenly spaced waves formed by winds far from the beach.

tar ball: A rounded mass of tar formed from the residue of an oil spill or seep. Sand and shells may stick to the surface of a tar ball, causing it to become armored.

tide: The twice-a-day (in North Carolina) elevation and depression of the local water level caused by the gravitational pull of the sun and moon on the ocean's waters as the earth rotates. High tide is the maximum elevation of the water level and low tide is the minimum level.

trough: The lowest point of a wave.

tsunami: An immense wave formed as the result of an earthquake, submarine landslide, or underwater volcanic eruption.

Vanderwaal forces: The weak electrical binding forces between sand grains and other grains and water in a natural dune.

volcano: An informal term for a small water/air extrusion feature on the surface of the beach that resembles a microvolcano. The cone is produced by sand grains extruded with the water.

water table: The surface of the zone of groundwater saturation.

wave: The form water takes as energy is transferred from the wind to the sea surface. Consisting of a crest (high point) and trough (low point), a wave moves through the water from its wind source to a coastline. Waves move water in a circular or elliptical rotation, not in a forward direction with the wave form.

wave amplitude: Half of the vertical distance between the wave crest and trough.

wave crest: The highest point of a wave.

wave frequency: The inverse of the wave period, or the fraction of a wave that passes a given point in one second.

wave height: The vertical distance between the wave crest and wave trough.

wavelength: The distance between wave crests.

wave orbital: The internal water movement caused by the passage of a wave. Orbitals are circular in deep water and elliptical in shallow water.

wave period: The time it takes for a wave crest to pass a given point.

wave ripples: Ripple marks formed by waves; also referred to as long-crested ripple marks.

wave setup: The piling up of water along a coastline by the continually incoming waves. Water brought in by waves comes in faster than it can drain back to sea, elevating the local water level during storms.

wet/dry beach line: The point on the beach where the intertidal zone (wet) part of the beach ends and the dry beach that does not get inundated at high tide starts.

wind ripple marks: Long-crested ripple marks formed by wind and usually of lower amplitude than water-wave ripples. Typically found on the back of the beach and in the sand dunes.

wind setup: The piling up of water along a coastline due to onshore winds. Winds blow water up against the beach, elevating the local water level, especially during storms, causing offshore flow of water along the sea floor.

wrack line: *See* drift line.

Suggested Readings

Alexander, J., and J. Lazell. *Ribbon of Sand: The Amazing Convergence of the Ocean and the Outer Banks.* Chapel Hill, N.C.: Algonquin Books, 1992. 238 pp. This book provides a casual view of barrier island environments of North Carolina.

Alongi, D. M. *Coastal Ecosystem Processes.* Boca Raton, Fla.: CRC Press, 1998. 419 pp. This manual contains a detailed summary of the meiofauna and nutrient cycles of beach and coastal ecosystems.

Au, S. *Vegetation and Ecological Processes on Shackleford Bank, North Carolina.* National Park Series Monograph No. 6. Washington, D.C.: GPO, 1974. 86 pp. This short volume summarizes the geology, ecology, climate, and physical environment of Shackleford Banks near Cape Lookout. A literature review of research conducted on the island is also included, as is a detailed discussion of the plants found here and their adaptations to their environment.

Barnes, J. *North Carolina's Hurricane History.* 3rd ed. Chapel Hill: University of North Carolina Press, 2001. 304 pp. This is a complete and thorough account of the hurricanes that have affected North Carolina throughout its history. Many photographs and firsthand stories give each hurricane a place in time and memory. The third edition includes all hurricanes through the 1990s.

Boschung, H., J. Williams, D. Gotshall, D. Caldwell, and M. Caldwell. *The Audubon Society Field Guide to North American Fishes, Whales, and Dolphins.* New York: Alfred A. Knopf, 1983. 848 pp. A detailed account of species of fishes and marine mammals of North America.

Bush, D. M., O. H. Pilkey Jr., and W. J. Neal. *Living by the Rules of the Sea.* Durham, N.C.: Duke University Press, 1996. 180 pp. This book provides a listing and discussion of the dynamic processes at the coast that every homeowner should know. Covering what happens during a storm, the hazards of living on a barrier island, how to mitigate property damages, and how to assess the risks at different places on the coast, this volume gives the coastal property owner or visitor the how-to's of living at the beach.

Davis, R. A., Jr. *The Evolving Coast.* New York: Scientific American Library, 1997. 233 pp. This well-illustrated primer is recommended as a global introduction to all types of coasts.

Davis, R. A., Jr., and D. FitzGerald. *Beaches and Coasts.* Oxford, Eng.:
Blackwell, 2003. 448 pp. Readers seeking a general textbook discussion of
beaches will enjoy this presentation by two of America's best coastal geologists.

Fox, W. T. *At the Sea's Edge: An Introduction to Coastal Oceanography for the
Amateur Naturalist.* New York: Prentice-Hall, 1983. 317 pp. Excellent
nontechnical, richly illustrated introduction to coastal processes, environment,
ecology, and meteorology.

Frankenberg, D. *The Nature of North Carolina's Southern Coast: Barrier Islands,
Coastal Waters, and Wetlands.* Chapel Hill: University of North Carolina
Press, 1997. 250 pp.

———. *The Nature of the Outer Banks: Environmental Processes, Field Sites, and
Development Issues, Corolla to Ocracoke.* Chapel Hill: University of North
Carolina Press, 1995. 157 pp. Together with the previous entry, this field
guide will take you to out-of-the-way places to enjoy natural habitats in North
Carolina's coastal zone.

Fussell, J. O., III. *Birder's Guide to Coastal North Carolina.* Chapel Hill: University of North Carolina Press, 1994. 540 pp. While looking at sedimentary
structures on the beach and dunes, you should still pay attention to the shells
and birds. John Fussell's birder's guide not only provides descriptions of birds
of special interest at the coast, but also tells you where to go and where to
look. Many of the tours outlined are in the vicinity of popular destinations
along North Carolina beaches.

Godfrey, P. J., and M. M. Godfrey. *Barrier Island Ecosystems of Cape Lookout
National Seashore and Vicinity, North Carolina.* National Park Service
Scientific Monograph No. 13. Washington, D.C.: GPO, 1977. This monograph describes studies of Core Banks that were conducted for several years
to detail the processes of overwash, plant response, and dune and marsh
development.

Graetz, K. E. *Seacoast Plants of the Carolinas.* 7th ed. University of North
Carolina Sea Grant Publication UNC-SG-73-06, 1994. 206 pp. A detailed
summary of the various plants found on the beaches and dunes of North and
South Carolina, including planting instructions for stabilization and protection of dunes.

Inman, D. L., and Dolan, R. "The Outer Banks of North Carolina: Budget of
Sediment and Inlet Dynamics along a Migrating Barrier System." *Journal of
Coastal Research* 5, no. 2 (1989): 193–238.

Kampion, D. *The Book of Waves: Form and Beauty on the Ocean.* 2nd ed.
Boulder, Colo.: Roberts Rinehart, 1997. 180 pp. A beautifully illustrated book

of waves from around the world, this volume also describes waves and how they form in easy-to-understand terms.

Kaplan, E. H. *A Field Guide to Southeastern and Caribbean Seashores: Cape Hatteras to the Gulf Coast, Florida, and the Caribbean.* Boston: Houghton Mifflin, 1988. 425 pp. One of the Peterson Field Guide series, sponsored by the National Audubon Society and the National Wildlife Federation, this book contains descriptions of most of the wildlife you are likely to come across in North Carolina.

Kaufman, W., and O. H. Pilkey Jr. *The Beaches Are Moving: The Drowning of America's Shoreline.* 7th ed. Durham, N.C.: Duke University Press, 1998. 336 pp. This account of the state of America's shoreline explains natural processes at work at the beach, provides a historical perspective of human-shoreline relations, and offers practical advice on how to live in harmony with the coastal environment.

Kraus, E. J. W. *A Guide to Ocean Dune Plants Common to North Carolina.* Chapel Hill: University of North Carolina Press, 1988. 72 pp. This short, illustrated guidebook summarizes the most common plants found on our state's dunes.

Lennon, G., W. J. Neal, D. M. Bush, O. H. Pilkey, M. Stutz, and J. Bullock. *Living with the South Carolina Coast.* Durham, N.C.: Duke University Press, 1996. 241 pp.

Mauldin, L., and D. Frankenberg. *North Carolina Marine Education Manual: Unit Three, Coastal Ecology.* University of North Carolina Sea Grant Publication UNC-SG-78-14-C, 1978. 100 pp. An education manual that discusses the plants and animals found all along North Carolina's coast, complete with exercises and experiments for children.

Meinkoth, N. *The Audubon Society Field Guide to North American Seashore Creatures.* New York: Alfred A. Knopf, 1981. 799 pp. A detailed summary of species and an overview of the taxonomy of major shore animals of North America, complete with color photographs.

Meyer, P. *Nature Guide to the Carolina Coast: Common Birds, Crabs, Shells, Fish and Other Entities of the Coastal Environment.* 4th ed. Wilmington, N.C.: Avian-Cetacean Press, 2001. 148 pp. This book is one of the most complete and thorough guidebooks to the various plants, shells, and animals in the state's coastal zone and includes many bright photographs for easy identification as you stroll along the beach. A must read for any budding naturalist.

Morris, G. *North Carolina Beaches.* Rev. and upd. ed. Chapel Hill: University of North Carolina Press, 1998. 312 pp. This travelers' guide is a road map to North Carolina's beaches as well as including interesting aspects of history, land use, the nature of the barrier islands, and the geomorphology of the coast.

Parnell, J. F., and M. A. Shields. *Management of North Carolina's Colonial Waterbirds.* University of North Carolina Sea Grant Publication UNC-SG-90-03, 1990. 169 pp. This Sea Grant book details the location and number of nesting birds along the marshes and islands of North Carolina's coast.

Pilkey, O. H., Jr., and K. L. Dixon. *The Corps and the Shore.* Washington, D.C.: Island Press, 1996. 272 pp. This book delves into the role of the U.S. Army Corps of Engineers in American beach management, including beach nourishment, and points out the need for external checks on Corps activities.

Pilkey, O. H., Jr., and M. E. Fraser. *A Celebration of the World's Barrier Islands.* New York: Columbia University Press, 2003. 309 pp. Coastal geologist Orrin Pilkey and artist/aerial photographer Mary Edna Fraser fuse science with art in this nontechnical, global view of barrier islands. The illustrated text provides insights into the variability of barrier islands, and although the inventory of islands is global in coverage, numerous examples are drawn from the Carolinas.

Pilkey, O. H., Jr., W. J. Neal, O. H. Pilkey Sr., and S. R. Riggs. *From Currituck to Calabash: Living with North Carolina's Barrier Islands.* Durham, N.C.: Duke University Press, 1980. 245 pp. The precursor to *The North Carolina Shore and Its Barrier Islands: Restless Ribbons of Sand,* this book was the first to cover the entire coast of the state in terms of discussing physical processes, recent history, and the relationship between man and the sea. The book describes each island in the state and provides recommendations on where and how to build along our coast.

Pilkey, O. H., Jr., W. J. Neal, S. R. Riggs, C. A. Webb, D. M. Bush, D. F. Pilkey, J. Bullock, and B. A. Cowan. *The North Carolina Shore and Its Barrier Islands: Restless Ribbons of Sand.* Durham, N.C.: Duke University Press, 1998. 319 pp. Arguing for a policy of intelligent shoreline development—one in which residential and commercial structures meet rather than confront the changing nature of the shore—this book presents practical information on hazards from storms, floods, erosion, island migration, and earthquakes. Construction guidelines, risk maps for each island, and discussions of controversies such as moving the Cape Hatteras Lighthouse and constructing a large jetty system at Oregon Inlet also are included.

Porter, H., and L. Houser. *Seashells of North Carolina.* University of North Carolina Sea Grant Publication No. UNC-SG-97-03, 1998. 132 pp. This reference book includes color and black-and-white photographs of more than 250 different shells found on our beaches, along with descriptions of each.

Rehder, H. A. *The Audubon Society Field Guide to North American Seashells*, New York: Alfred A. Knopf, 1981. 894 pp. This well-illustrated reference is an excellent handbook for the serious shell collector.

Schoenbaum, T. J. *Islands, Capes, and Sounds: The North Carolina Coast.* Winston-Salem, N.C.: John F. Blair, 1982. 332 pp. This publication provides a history of the Outer Banks and the early settlements along Albemarle and Pamlico Sounds.

Spitsbergen, J. M. *Seacoast Life.* Chapel Hill: University of North Carolina Press, 1983. 112 pp. This book provides good illustrations and descriptions of the flora and fauna found on the barrier islands of North Carolina.

Stick, D. *The Outer Banks of North Carolina.* Chapel Hill: University of North Carolina Press, 1958. 352 pp. This classic history of the Outer Banks is recommended to all residents of coastal North Carolina, particularly those in Carteret, Hyde, and Currituck Counties. Contains storm history, accounts of the origins of most points of interest, and examples of early development.

Woodroffe, C. D. *Coasts: Form, Process and Evolution.* New York: Cambridge University Press, 2003. 638 pp. Although this is a technical text, the author introduces a wide range of topics including coastal types and their classifications; tides, currents, and waves; cliffed coasts; beaches, spits, and barrier islands; changing sea levels; coastal dunes; deltas; estuaries and lagoons; and coral reefs.

Index